Argentina
and the Fund:
From Triumph
to Tragedy

Argentina and the Fund: From Triumph to Tragedy

Michael Mussa

Institute for International Economics
Washington, DC
July 2002

Michael Mussa, senior fellow, served as economic counselor and director of the Department of Research at the International Monetary Fund from 1991–2001, where he was responsible for advising the management of the Fund and the Fund's Executive Board on broad issues of economic policy and for providing analysis of ongoing developments in the world economy. He served as a member of the US Council of Economic Advisers from August 1986 to September 1988. He was a member of the faculty of the Graduate School of Business at the University of Chicago (1976–91) and was on the faculty of the Department of Economics at the University of Rochester (1971–76). During this period he also served as a visiting faculty member at the Graduate Center of the City University of New York, the London School of Economics, and the Graduate Institute of International Studies in Geneva, Switzerland. He has published widely on macroeconomics, monetary economics, international economics, and municipal finance in professional journals and research volumes.

INSTITUTE FOR INTERNATIONAL ECONOMICS
1750 Massachusetts Avenue, NW
Washington, DC 20036-1903
(202) 328-9000   FAX: (202) 659-3225
http://www.iie.com

C. Fred Bergsten, *Director*
Brigitte Coulton, *Director of Publications and Web Development*
Brett Kitchen, *Director of Marketing*

Printing by Victor Graphics, Inc.
Typesetting by BMWW

Printed in the United States of America
03 02 01   5 4 3 2 1

Library of Congress Cataloging-in-Publication Data

Mussa, Michael.
  Argentina and the Fund : from triumph to tragedy / Michael Mussa.
    p. cm.
  Includes bibliographical references and index.
    ISBN 0-88132-339-X

  1. International Monetary Fund—Argentina.   2. Fiscal policy—Argentina.
  3. Argentina—Economic policy.   I. Title

HG3881.5 .I58 M87 2002
332.1'52'0982—dc21   2002068630

The views expressed in this publication are those of the author. This publication is part of the overall program of the Institute, as endorsed by its Board of Directors, but does not necessarily reflect the views of individual members of the Board or the Advisory Committee.

From

Widener

Harvard University Library
Messenger Service

Harvard University Library
Messenger Service

From

Date
Stamp

Deliver to

Contents

5 Lessons for the Fund

Preface

This analysis of the unfolding tragedy of Argentina, written during the spring of 2002 as that country sought to emerge from its deepest postwar crisis, addresses at least five major themes of the current debate on the functioning of the international monetary system.

First and foremost, it assesses the story of Argentina itself. How could the country which became the darling of both the financial markets and the global policy community for almost a decade, as a poster child of desirable reform, fall back into deep and prolonged recession? Why did default and devaluation become necessary? What went wrong?

Second, what was the role of the International Monetary Fund in this collapse? With Argentina under its tutelage throughout the period under review, doesn't the Fund bear substantial responsibility for what happened? Did it fail to provide proper prudential advice while times were good? Did its counsel, or lack thereof, contribute to the subsequent fall? Did it provide too much money or too little money—or both, at different times?

Third, what does the Argentine experience teach us about the operations of the Fund itself? Are the dynamics of its internal procedures and deliberations likely to produce objective and balanced assessments of country situations as a basis for sound policy decisions? Or do its own institutional goals and unique structures predispose it to actions that may be ineffectual, or even counterproductive, in resolving difficult situations?

Fourth, what was the role of Argentina's currency board both in the initial success and the ultimate collapse of its efforts to achieve and maintain both price stability and economic success? Was the mechanism flawed or was it the implementation that failed in this case? Can general lessons be drawn concerning this particular approach to national economic management, which has attracted considerable attention in recent years and been either adopted or considered for adoption in a number of countries?

Fifth, are there broader lessons for reform of the "international financial architecture?" Did generous IMF support for Argentina, including when it was already close to crisis in late 2001, reinforce the view that official bailouts are inevitable and thus intensify the "moral hazard" that some observers believe represents a major flaw in the current system?

Few authors are as well placed to address these questions as Michael Mussa, who became a Senior Fellow at the Institute in the fall of 2001. He had spent the previous ten years as Economic Counselor and Director of Research at the International Monetary Fund, where he was responsible for advising the management of the Fund and the Fund's Executive Board on broad issues of economic policy and for providing analysis of ongoing developments in the world economy. Dr. Mussa was thus closely involved in the evolution of the Fund's policy toward Argentina for most of the period covered by this study. His assessments of the role of the Fund and the impact of its decision-making mechanisms, while not a "kiss and tell" account, are thus particularly insightful and valuable. His conclusion that the Fund's last pre-crisis loan to Argentina in August 2001 was "the greatest mistake the Fund made in my ten years there" is thus of considerable importance to the ongoing debate over this crucial and tragic case.

The Institute for International Economics is a private nonprofit institution for the study and discussion of international economic policy. Its purpose is to analyze important issues in that area and to develop and communicate practical new approaches for dealing with them. The Institute is completely nonpartisan.

The Institute is funded largely by philanthropic foundations. Major institutional grants are now being received from the William M. Keck, Jr. Foundation and the Starr Foundation. A number of other foundations and private corporations contribute to the highly diversified financial resources of the Institute. About 31 percent of the Institute's resources in our latest fiscal year were provided by contributors outside the United States, including about 18 percent from Japan.

The Board of Directors bears overall responsibilities for the Institute and gives general guidance and approval to its research program, including the identification of topics that are likely to become important over the medium run (one to three years), and which should be addressed by the Institute. The Director, working closely with the staff and outside Advisory Committee, is responsible for the development of particular projects and makes the final decision to publish an individual study.

The Institute hopes that its studies and other activities will contribute to building a stronger foundation for international economic policy around the world. We invite readers of these publications to let us know how they think we can best accomplish this objective.

C. FRED BERGSTEN
Director
June 2002

Acknowledgments

The author would like to thank his colleagues at the Institute for International Economics, especially C. Fred Bergsten, Morris Goldstein, Bill Cline, and Ted Truman, as well as several former colleagues at the International Monetary Fund, for their useful comments on earlier drafts of this policy analysis.

The author would also like to thank Pavel Trcala for his research assistance, and the editorial and production staff of the Institute for their expeditious work in preparing the manuscript for publication.

1

Introduction: Setting the Stage

In the sad economic history of Argentina during the past half-century, the past decade encompassed a remarkable transition. Rising from the ashes of yet another episode of economic chaos and hyperinflation at the end of the 1980s, the surprisingly orthodox policies of the new Peronist president, Carlos Menem, brought a decisive end to decades of monetary instability and launched the Argentine economy into four years of unusually rapid and sustained expansion. Those economic policies, which were largely the brainchild of President Menem's formidable economy minister, Domingo Cavallo, featured a hard peg of the Argentine peso at parity to the US dollar, backed by the Convertibility Plan, which strictly limited domestic money creation under an arrangement similar to a currency board.

Many doubted whether the new policy regime would survive, especially as tensions rose during the tequila crisis initiated by the Mexican devaluation of December 1994. But it did survive; and after a sharp recession in 1995 (and persistently high unemployment thereafter), the Argentine economy resumed rapid growth from late 1995 until the spillover effects of the Brazilian crisis hit Argentina in late 1998. Indeed, with most of the miracle economies of emerging Asia collapsing into crises from mid-1997 to early 1998, Argentina became the darling of emerging-market finance—able to float large issues of medium-term and long-term debt on world credit markets at comparatively modest spreads over US Treasuries. And in the official international financial community, especially the International Monetary Fund, many of Argentina's economic policies were widely applauded and suggested as a model that other emerging-market countries should emulate—international approval that was dramatized by President Menem's triumphant address to the IMF-World Bank Annual Meetings on 4 October 1998.

Barely three years later, Argentina's decade-long experiment with hard money and orthodox policies has ended in tragedy—the depths of which are not yet fully known. The economy is well into its fourth year of recession and rapidly spiraling downward. Most of the banking system has effectively been closed since the beginning of December 2001, and there is no indication of when it may resume something approaching normal operations. The exchange rate peg is gone, and the peso is trading at substantially depreciated exchange rates against the dollar. Economic and financial chaos—banished from Argentina since the hyperinflation of 1990—have returned, and there is a real threat that hyperinflation itself may soon return unless the Argentine authorities can rapidly reestablish and maintain credible monetary and fiscal discipline. With formal default on its sovereign external debt, Argentina has been transformed within barely two years from the darling of emerging-market finance to the world's leading deadbeat.

Focus on the Role of the Fund

These developments, of course, mainly concern the Argentine people. It is they who feel the great pain of the current tragedy. It is their government that designed and pursued the policies that led both to this tragedy and to the substantial successes that were achieved earlier. And it is their government, with their support, that has the responsibility to find a way out of the present morass. However, the international community, both official and private, played a significant role in the economic evolution of Argentina during the past decade; and it should seek to play a constructive role going forward. Indeed, the purpose of this policy analysis is primarily to examine the role of the International Monetary Fund, and of the international community more broadly, in Argentina's transition from triumph to tragedy during the past decade.

The Argentine case is important for understanding the Fund because Argentina is an important country and dealing with its present difficulties poses a substantial challenge for the international community. Moreover, the way critical issues are dealt with in the Argentine case, notably the resolution of Argentina's sovereign default, will undoubtedly set important precedents that will influence the future functioning of the international financial system.

More than this, however, the Argentine case is particularly revealing because the Fund was deeply involved with Argentina for many years before the emergence of the present crisis. In this important respect, Argentina is different from most other cases where the Fund has provided exceptionally large financial support. Virtually continuously throughout the 1990s, Argentina operated under the auspices and close scrutiny of a Fund-supported program. In contrast, in other cases where the Fund provided exceptionally large support (Mexico in 1995; Indonesia, South Korea, and Thailand in the Asian crisis; Brazil in the crisis of late 1998 and early 1999), a Fund-supported program was started only after the crisis was already under way.

Thus, any failures of the Fund in the pre-crisis period were those of its relatively low-intensity surveillance activities. For Argentina, the failures of the Fund are clearly associated with the core of the Fund's most intense involvement with a member: when it is providing financial assistance and when the policies and performance of the member are subject to the intense scrutiny of Fund conditionality. Leaving aside Turkey, where the outcome is not yet clear, the only other case of exceptionally large Fund financing to a member already operating under a Fund-supported program was Russia in the summer of 1998. But Russia was a very special case. The Fund (and the rest of the international financial community) faced the new challenge of assisting a country involved in the transition from a socialist to a market economy; and there were intense political concerns in the Russian case that spread well beyond the economic and financial sphere.

For Argentina, these additional concerns were by no means as intense. Moreover, in Russia and in the countries caught up in the Asian crisis, the key policy issues involved deep problems of structural reform (including problems of financial sector) that passed beyond the Fund's established areas of competence. In contrast, the economic issues that Argentina needed to confront were primarily in the areas of fiscal, monetary, and exchange rate policy—the traditional bread and butter of Fund policy concerns. Thus, to the extent that the Fund got it wrong, or failed to get it right, in Argentina, this is likely to be revealing of particularly deep-seated deficiencies.

Necessarily, the emphasis here must be on issues where the Fund got it wrong in Argentina. This does not imply that the Fund got it completely wrong or that the Fund, rather than the Argentine authorities, was primarily responsible for the ultimate outcome. However, the end result in Argentina has clearly been a disaster of considerable magnitude. This disaster was certainly not intended or, until relatively recently, broadly anticipated—by the Argentine authorities, the Fund, or anyone else.

No reasonable person, however, should believe that substantially better outcomes were not achievable under realistic alternative economic policies if they had been implemented sufficiently early and appropriately vigorously. And, in view of the Fund's deep and continuing involvement with Argentina's economic policies, its financial support for those policies, and the confidence in and praise for those policies that the Fund so often expressed, it follows that the Fund must bear responsibility for the mistakes that it made in this important case; and it must be prepared to recognize and learn from these mistakes.

I shall argue that the Fund did make at least two important mistakes in Argentina: (1) in failing to press the Argentine authorities much harder to have a more responsible fiscal policy, especially during the high growth years of the early through mid 1990s; and (2) in extending substantial additional financial support to Argentina during the summer of 2001, after it had become abundantly clear that the Argentine government's efforts to avoid default and maintain the exchange rate peg had no reasonable chance of success.

I shall also discuss three other important issues where it might reasonably be argued that the Fund got it wrong but for which, in view of the Fund's particular mandate and responsibilities vis-à-vis its members, it did take the right position: (1) the initial skepticism at the Fund about the desirability and viability of the exchange rate peg before the tequila crisis; (2) the Fund's subsequent support for the Argentine decision to maintain the peg; and (3) the decision by the Fund in December 2000 (formally approved by the Executive Board in early 2001) to organize a large international financial support package to assist Argentina at a time when a number of competent observers were concerned that such a large support package was not appropriate.

To develop the basis for the analysis of these issues, it is essential to review key aspects of the economic evolution of Argentina during the past decade. In particular, because sovereign default was clearly a critical factor in provoking the present catastrophe, it is important to understand how the Argentine government proceeded from a situation of apparent solvency—reflected in its ability to float large volumes of debt in international financial markets—to the point where it could no longer service its obligations. And, given the Fund's traditional emphasis on fiscal probity, it is important to discuss what the Fund was saying and doing as Argentina's fiscal situation deteriorated.

It is also clear that the collapse of Argentina's Convertibility Plan in late 2001 played a central role in the present crisis. Accordingly, it is critical to examine both how the Convertibility Plan contributed to the initial success of Argentina's stabilization and reform efforts and why the plan ultimately collapsed in tragedy. Moreover, as with Argentina's fiscal policy, it is important to discuss what the Fund was saying and doing about Argentina's monetary and exchange rate policy, both as the crisis loomed and at an earlier stage when a more orderly shift away from the Convertibility Plan might have been undertaken.

During 2000 and 2001, as the threat of a catastrophic crisis clearly deepened, the Argentine government undertook increasingly urgent and desperate measures to try to head off that crisis. The Fund supported these efforts with exceptionally large financial packages, despite deep concerns of many in the international community about the usefulness and appropriateness of such packages. These efforts clearly failed catastrophically—giving rise to the question of whether they were wise in the first place, or whether an earlier decision to accept the inevitable might have led to a less disastrous outcome.

Looking to the future rather than the past, it also seems relevant to examine what Argentina needs to emerge as rapidly and successfully as possible from the present crisis, and what the Fund and the international community can and should do to assist Argentina in this endeavor. In addition, because experience is the most effective teacher and the lessons from failure may be even more valuable than those from success, it is appropriate to reflect on the lessons that Argentina may teach about the Fund and how it might better fulfill its responsibilities in the international monetary and financial system. Before turning to these issues, however, it is essential to state one important qualification about what is said in this book.

An Essential Qualification

A good deal has already been written and said in the media about the crisis in Argentina and the role played by the Fund; and much more will be said. Most commentators, both journalists and economists, have been careful so far to emphasize one critical point about the policies that ultimately led to the crisis: they were the policies desired and implemented by the Argentine government. In general, the Fund supported these policies, both with its statements and with its financing, but the Fund did not press the Argentine government to adopt policies that it did not willingly choose to implement.

This is especially true in what proved to be the two most important areas of Argentine economic policy: monetary and exchange rate policy, and fiscal policy. In fact, the initial decision to adopt the Convertibility Plan—which rigidly linked the peso at parity to the US dollar and tightly constrained monetary policy to support the exchange rate peg—was made by the Argentine government against the advice of the Fund. Many of the Fund's staff (myself included) remained highly skeptical about this policy through the mid-1990s. After the arrangement survived the tequila crisis (thanks to particularly effective policy management by the Argentine authorities and with moderate financial support from the Fund), the attitude in the Fund generally shifted to support for the arrangement.

Subsequent decisions to persist with the Convertibility Plan, especially as it came under increasing pressure during the period 1999–2001, were clearly the choice of the Argentine authorities. These decisions were supported by the Fund. But there should be no doubt that if the Argentines had decided to move to an alternative, more flexible exchange rate and monetary policy regime that maintained reasonable monetary discipline, this would also have been acceptable to the Fund. Indeed, at least some in the Fund (although probably not a majority at the time) would have welcomed serious consideration of such a move by the Argentine authorities.

In the area of fiscal policy, the persistent running of significant fiscal deficits and the consequent increases in the stock of government debt were clearly the result of decisions by the Argentine authorities. In accord with its usual preferences, the Fund would have generally favored smaller deficits and less debt buildup. In the policies adopted to meet the challenge of the tequila crisis, the Fund did (as usual) press for a tighter fiscal stance to reassure Argentina's somewhat nervous creditors. The Fund was also understanding (to an unusual extent by previous standards) when the fiscal position deteriorated more than anticipated during 1995 because the economy was weaker than had been expected.

During the next three years, the Argentine economy generally recovered more rapidly than was envisioned in the Fund-supported programs. This should easily have allowed the Argentine authorities to achieve smaller fiscal deficits than were allowed for in these programs. Instead, the Argentine authorities chose to run slightly larger deficits (in nominal terms) than permitted by the program targets. In addition, there was a buildup of government debt (including provincial debt) that, for a variety of reasons, was not included in the deficit targets. In this period, as a result of the actions of the Argentine authorities, the cumulative buildup of government debt was significantly larger than the Fund expected and would have liked to see.

During the period 2000–01, as doubts grew about the ability of Argentina to service its growing debt burden and sustain its exchange rate peg, the new Argentine authorities decided to adopt austerity measures to attempt to reduce the fiscal deficit and thereby reassure creditors. The Fund supported these measures. In fact, the conditionality associated with the large support package of December 2000 insisted on fiscal polices that would significantly reduce the deficit—despite the ongoing recession in Argentina. The Argentine authorities accepted that such measures were essential to meet their objectives of avoiding the devastating consequences of default and/or devaluation.

As the crisis deepened during the course of 2001 and the deficit targets set in the Fund-supported program were missed, the Argentine authorities sought to undertake further austerity measures. The Fund supported these efforts as essential to meet the key objectives set by the Argentine authorities. However, had the Argentine authorities decided at some time during 2000–01 (before the collapse in December 2001) to pursue an alternative course involving debt restructuring and a possible change in the exchange rate regime, the Fund would have supported responsible efforts in this direction.

At the Fund, there has been much recent discussion of the importance of "ownership" of Fund-supported programs—in the sense that the authorities fully accept the necessity and desirability of the policy measures that they have agreed on with the Fund. Sometimes in Fund-supported programs, ownership is a problem, especially when the Fund presses (on behalf of the international community) for policies that raise domestic political difficulties.

Policy ownership was not an issue in Argentina during the past decade. For better or worse, all the key policies were fully owned by the Argentine authorities. Accordingly, if the Fund made important mistakes in Argentina—as I believe it did—they must have been primarily sins of omission: either failures of the Fund to press hard enough and soon enough for policies of the Argentine government that would have been likely to improve the outcome; or failures of the Fund to discourage sufficiently forcefully policies that exacerbated the tragedy.

2

What Went Wrong in Argentina

Several factors contributed to the remarkable deterioration of Argentina from an apparent paragon of economic reform and stabilization in 1997–98 to the tragedy now unfolding in that economy. If Argentina had a more flexible economic system, especially in its labor markets, its economy would have been more able to adapt to the rigors of the Convertibility Plan; unemployment would have been lower; growth would have been stronger; fiscal deficits would have been smaller; and interest rates would have been lower because creditors would have had more confidence in the capacity of the Argentine government to service its obligations.

Moreover, if the US dollar had not been so strong in recent years, Argentina would have had a more competitive exchange rate vis-à-vis its important European trading partners, contributing both to somewhat better growth and a better balance of payments. If Argentina had not suffered the external shock from the collapse of Brazil's crawling-peg exchange rate policy, one of the important causes of Argentina's recession during the period 1999–2001 would have been removed; and this would have had favorable consequences in several important dimensions. Or if Argentina had decided in 1997 or 1998 that the Convertibility Plan had fulfilled its purpose and the time had come to shift to a more flexible regime for exchange rate and monetary policy, it might have been better able to manage the difficulties of 1999–2001. In sum, if things had broken more in Argentina's favor, this surely would have helped to preserve the success and avoid the tragedy of Argentina's stabilization efforts.

An Unsustainable Fiscal Policy

Enumerating the many things that contributed to Argentina's tragedy, however, should not obscure the critical, avoidable failure of Argentine economic policy that was the fundamental cause of disaster—namely, the chronic inability of the Argentine authorities to maintain a responsible fiscal policy. This is an old, sad story for Argentina. To satisfy various political needs and pressures, the government (at all levels) has a persistent tendency to spend significantly more than can be raised in taxes. When the government can finance its excess spending with borrowing, it borrows domestically or internationally from wherever credit is available. When further borrowing is no longer feasible (either to finance current deficits or roll over outstanding debts), recourse is found in inflationary money creation and/or explicit default and expropriation of creditors.

This is what happened during the presidency of Raul Alfonsin, culminating in the hyperinflation of 1990. With some differences in the details but none in the central substance, it is also what happened in the events that culminated in several earlier financial crises during the preceding 50 years. Thus, in the management of its fiscal affairs, the Argentine government is like a chronic alcoholic—once it starts to imbibe the political pleasures of deficit spending, it keeps on going until in reaches the economic equivalent of falling-down drunk.

This is what happened again during the past decade—and on a scale that surpassed even Argentina's past accomplishments in the dubious domain of fiscal irresponsibility. To appreciate what happened, it is useful to recall that the 1980s were a very poor decade for the Argentine economy; see figure 2.1. Indeed, the index of real GDP reached its peak for the decade in 1980, then declined by 10 percent by 1985, and subsequently recovered to just below its 1980 peak in 1987. A deep recession followed, amid financial instability that culminated in the hyperinflation of 1990, with real GDP ultimately falling more than 10 percent below its 1987 level. The inflation at the end of the decade wiped out much of the domestic currency debt of the Argentine government, leaving the dollar-denominated external debt as the bulk of the $80 billion face value of debt outstanding in 1990. The face value of the debt was reduced by about $10 billion in the Brady bond restructuring of early 1993. This left the Argentine government with a debt-to-GDP ratio of 29 percent in 1993.

The Convertibility Plan was introduced at the start of April 1991. As is often the case with exchange-rate-based stabilizations, it helped to bring both a precipitous reduction of inflation, down to the low single digits by 1993, and a remarkable rebound in economic activity, with the index of real GDP rising by 28 percent cumulatively between 1990 and 1993. It is not surprising, with such a spectacular recovery of the economy, that the Argentine government was able to maintain a fiscal policy that avoided increases in the outstanding stock of government debt. However, the

Figure 2.1 Real economic indicators for Argentina, 1960–91

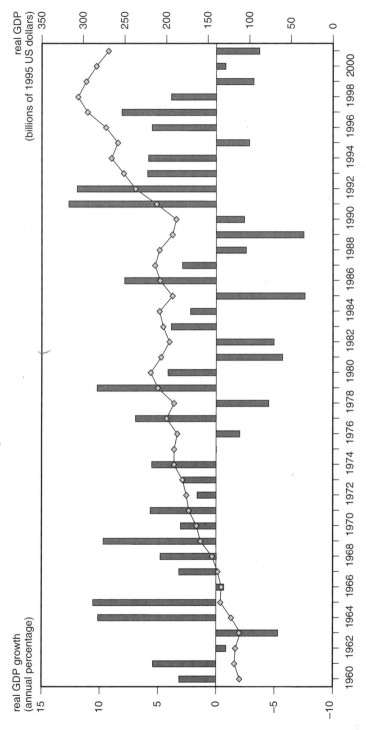

real GDP growth
(annual percentage)

real GDP
(billions of 1995 US dollars)

Note: The bars trace real GDP growth (left axis) and the line traces real GDP (right axis).

Sources: IMF *World Economic Outlook* database and Economic Ministry of Argentina.

Table 2.1 Selected economic indicators for Argentina, 1993–98

Indicator	1993	1994	1995	1996	1997	1998
GDP (billions of US dollars)	237	257	258	272	293	299
Real GDP (percent change)	5.7	5.8	−2.8	5.5	8.1	3.9
Central government budget balance (percent of GDP)	0.9	−0.5	−1.4	−2.2	−1.6	−1.3
Consolidated government budget balance (percent of GDP)	−0.2	−1.7	−3.4	−3.3	−2.1	−2.1
Total public debt (percent of GDP)	29.2	31.1	35.9	37.7	38.9	41.4

Sources: Nominal GDP and percentage change in real GDP were calculated by the author from data in the IMF *International Financial Statistics Yearbook 2001*; other data are from IMF Press Release 96/15, April 12, 1996, and from IMF Public Information Notice 00/84, October 3, 2000.

growth rates of the Argentine economy during the initial years of recovery from the disaster of the 1980s were clearly not sustainable, and the real test of Argentine fiscal policy would come when economic growth slowed to a more sustainable pace—as occurred between 1993 and 1998.

Table 2.1 presents some relevant indicators. Using the annual average data on which this table is based, the change between 1993 and 1998 corresponds essentially to the change during the five years from mid-1993 (after the Argentine economy was past the initial stage of very rapid recovery) to mid-1998 (before the Argentine economy fell into the recession at the end of the decade). This five-year period includes the sharp recession associated with the tequila crisis of 1995, as was reflected in a 2.8 percent year-over-year decline of real GDP between 1994 and 1995. Otherwise, however, the Argentine economy enjoyed quite strong growth, as well as very low inflation, during this period.

Indeed, notwithstanding the tequila crisis recession, Argentina's real GDP advanced at an annual average rate of 4.4 percent between 1993 and 1998. Aside from brief growth spurts in recoveries following financial crises, this growth record was by far the best performance of the Argentine economy since the 1960s, as is illustrated by the real GDP growth of the Argentine economy on a five-year moving average basis; see figure 2.2. With the GDP deflator rising less than 3 percent cumulatively between 1993 and 1998, the rise in nominal GDP was only modestly larger than the rise in real GDP, but it still recorded a solid cumulative gain of 26 percent between 1993 and 1998.

How was Argentine fiscal policy performing during this period of generally superior economic performance? The central-government budget balance (as a share of GDP) was the measure usually given greatest importance in International Monetary Fund programs. The central-government budget recorded a small surplus in 1993 and was in moderate deficit thereafter. Taken at face value, these budget results do not look too bad, espe-

Figure 2.2 Real GDP growth for Argentina (5-year moving average), **1964–2001**

annual percentage

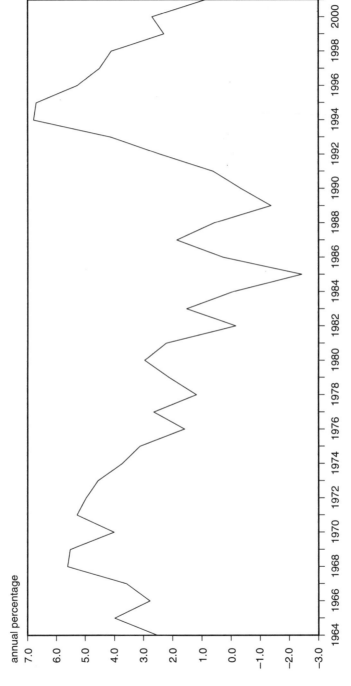

Sources: Economic Ministry of Argentina and author's calculations.

cially if one recognizes that the tequila-crisis recession tended to boost the deficit in 1995–96.

However, even restricting attention to the central government, the fiscal outcome in these generally high-growth years was significantly worse than it initially appears. From 1993 through 1998, the Argentine central government realized $3.1 billion of nonrecurring revenues from the proceeds of privatization and another $1.4 billion of capital account revenues that offset what would otherwise have been an increase in the government debt of another 2 percent of GDP.

More important, the Brady bond restructuring involved a substantial back-loading of interest payments. This is reflected in the fact the central government's interest payments on its external debt rose from $2.6 billion in 1993 to $6.4 billion in 1998. A modest part of this nearly $4 billion increase in interest expense is attributable to increases in the stock of debt between 1993 and 1998; but most of it reflects deferral of interest expense that is effectively a disguised form of government borrowing. And the further increase in interest expense on the external debt up to $10.2 billion by 2001 also partly reflects the effects of deferring earlier interest expense. Moreover, many of Argentina's fiscal problems (particularly in the 1990s but also at earlier times) arose from inadequate fiscal discipline in the provinces, for which the central government ultimately had to take responsibility. Indeed, the Argentine system—enshrined in the Constitution and in decades of practice—was fundamentally one in which the provinces retained much of the initiative and incentive for public spending, but the responsibility for raising of revenue and payment of debt was passed off largely to the central government. The operation of this system of fiscal irresponsibility is reflected in the figures for the consolidated government budget balance, which incorporates all levels of government. Every year the budget balance for the consolidated government is significantly worse than for the central government alone.

If public-sector borrowing in a given year corresponded to the consolidated government deficit in that year, as one might naively expect from standard accounting principles, then the cumulative increase in public debt during several years would correspond to the cumulative consolidated government deficit during those years. In fact, the ratio of total public debt to GDP in Argentina rose from 29.2 to 41.4 percent between 1993 and 1998—an increase in the debt-to-GDP ratio of 12.2 percentage points. This looks quite close to the sum of the ratios of consolidated budget deficit to GDP during this period—either 12.8 percent including 1993 or 12.6 percent excluding 1993. However, the denominator in the ratio of debt to GDP, nominal GDP, rose 26 percent between 1993 and 1998; and this should have depressed the gain in the debt-to-GDP ratio by about 7 percentage points below the sum of the deficit-to-GDP ratio results for these years. Why not? Because the Argentine public sector engaged in a good deal of borrowing that was not included in the budget; see figure 2.3.

Figure 2.3 Fiscal deficit and change in public debt

billions of US dollars

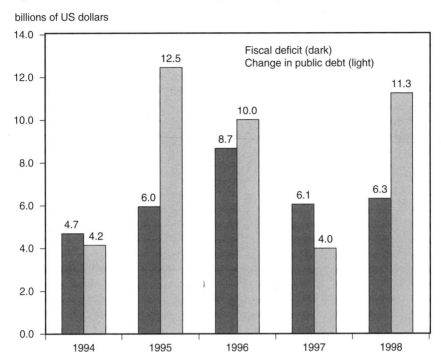

Source: Economic Ministry of Argentina.

For some purposes, such as judging the likely effect of deficit spending on aggregate demand, it may be appropriate to exclude some components of public-sector borrowing from a relevant measure of the budget deficit. To assess overall budget discipline and fiscal sustainability, however, pubic debt is public debt, and all of it counts. Thus, at the bottom line, the fiscal results for the Argentine public sector during 1993 to 1998 show an increase in the debt-to-GDP ratio of 12 percentage points. If Argentine fiscal policy produced this large an increase in the debt-to-GDP ratio during a period of superior economic performance, what might it reasonably be expected to produce in less favorable circumstances?

Indeed, as was noted above, Argentina's fiscal performance in 1993–98 was actually worse than is suggested by this rhetorical question. During this period, Argentina's fiscal performance benefited from the Brady bond deal in terms of the back-loading of interest payments, as well as the Argentine government's receipt of significant privatization and other capital revenues that were fully counted on budget. *In sum, during the period 1993–98, when the Argentine economy was generally performing very well and the Argentine government was receiving substantial nonrecurring revenues from privatization and enjoyed other temporary fiscal benefits, the public-sector debt-to-GDP ratio nevertheless rose by 12 percentage points. This clearly was not an adequately disciplined or sustainable fiscal policy.*

Because most industrial countries have government debt-to-GDP ratios above 50 percent and some above 100 percent, it might be asked why a debt-to-GDP ratio of just above 40 percent was worrying for Argentina. There are at least five important reasons.

First, unlike some industrial countries that successfully carry much higher debt-to-GDP ratios, Argentina has had little success in raising tax revenues (including social security contributions) of more than 20 percent of GDP, compared with nearly 50 percent of GDP in several European countries. Indeed, in Argentina, the provinces are perennially in deficit and, from time to time, have called on the central government to assume responsibility for their debts. Thus, as a practical matter, any revenue of the provinces is committed to spending and little of it is likely to be available for debt service. This means that the tax base that realistically might be available to pay debt service is the tax revenue of the central government, less the substantial funds that legally must be transferred to the provinces.

Second, with most of its government debt denominated in foreign currency and with much of this debt held externally, Argentina faced the dual challenge of persuading creditors that it was capable both of raising sufficient fiscal revenues to service its debt and of being able to convert these revenues into foreign exchange with an exchange rate that was rigidly pegged to the US dollar. In addition, the Argentine private sector had significant external foreign-currency debt which required foreign exchange for its servicing. Indeed, Argentina's total external debt rose massively from $62 billion at the end of 1992 to $142 billion by the end of 1998—more than doubling during a period when Argentina's nominal GDP rose by about a quarter.

Traditionally, export receipts are taken as a measure of the foreign exchange earnings that might be available to service a country's external debts. As is the case with many countries that substantially reduce their barriers to external trade, Argentina's trade expanded rapidly from 1993 to 1998, with both exports and imports doubling. The rapid expansion of exports helped to limit the rise in the ratio of external debt to exports. Nevertheless, at more than 400 percent, this ratio was exceptionally high relative to that of most countries—at a level that often signals a substantial risk of an external financing crisis that can only be resolved through debt restructuring.

Third, it is not just the level of the government debt (relative to GDP or tax revenues or exports) that matters; it is also how the debt has been behaving. If Argentina had stabilized its debt-to-GDP ratio for some time, under both good and bad economic conditions, then a debt-to-GDP ratio around 40 percent might not have been so worrying. However, a debt-to-GDP ratio that rose from 29 to 41 percent of GDP during generally good economic times was surely a worrying signal of incapacity to maintain reasonable fiscal discipline, especially for a country with a record of persistent difficulties in this area.

Fourth, emerging-market countries in general, and Argentina especially, was potentially vulnerable to external economic shocks that might impair fiscal sustainability at debt-to-GDP ratios far lower than those of industrial countries. Indeed, this is what happened. Events surrounding the collapse of Brazil's crawling-peg exchange rate in early 1999 had important negative spillovers for Argentina. Real GDP contracted 4 percent between 1998 and 2000. The price level also fell, with the result that nominal GDP dropped 4.9 percent between 1998 and 2000. In this weak economic environment, despite some efforts at fiscal consolidation, the budget deficit widened. With public debt rising and nominal GDP falling, the debt-to-GDP ratio jumped from 41 percent in 1998 to 50 percent in 2000. With recession and deflation continuing in 2001, the economic and political environment for fiscal consolidation was clearly becoming even more difficult; and there was real reason to fear that the public debt was on an unsustainable upward spiral.

Fifth, as an emerging-market country with substantial external debt, Argentina was clearly vulnerable to changes in financial market sentiment. Aside from brief interruptions during periods of general market turmoil, Argentina would probably be able to maintain necessary access to external financing—as long as financial markets believed it was a good credit risk. However, its long record of periodic financial crises and debt restructurings was not reassuring. If market sentiment ever shifted to an expectation of significant risk that Argentina might default, its market access would be cut off and that expectation would soon become self-fulfilling.

The Fund and Fiscal Policy

What was the International Monetary Fund's role in the fiscal failures of the Argentine government? As was noted above, aside from showing some understanding about the difficulties of tightening fiscal policy in the midst of the tequila crisis, the Fund clearly did not encourage the Argentine government to run up large deficits and build up its debt to the point of nonsustainability. However, the Fund did fail to press the Argentine authorities as hard as it could have and should have to maintain a more prudent fiscal policy. Why not?

In the period from 1991 through the start of the tequila crisis, fiscal policy was not the Fund's most urgent concern for Argentina. The excess of government spending over recurring revenues was modest and was financed partly by privatization receipts and other sources that did not lead immediately to increases in debt; and the level of government debt was not threatening. The central concern was that the exchange rate, which was pegged at parity to the US dollar in nominal terms, was becoming overvalued in real terms because inflation in Argentina (although dramatically reduced) remained above US inflation. Also, as the Argentine economy recovered from the economic impact of hyperinflation, domestic expenditure rose sharply, contributing to a growing current account deficit. The key concern was that if the capital flows to Argentina that were financing the current account deficit began to reverse or even slow down significantly, a foreign exchange crisis would likely ensue.

Indeed, I recall expressing the concern in the autumn of 1994 that a foreign exchange crisis starting in Argentina would probably also take down the Mexican peso. It happened the other way around; the tequila crisis started with the devaluation of the Mexican peso in mid-December 1994 and spread quickly to Argentina. The Fund supported Argentina's successful efforts to maintain its exchange rate peg in that crisis. The policy response included a moderate tightening of fiscal policy, intended both to contribute to a reduction in the current account deficit and to reassure Argentina's creditors.

When the actual fiscal deficit began to exceed the program targets during 1995 because of an economy that was weaker than expected, the Fund insisted on some further tightening measures; but it showed unusual flexibility (by past Fund standards) in allowing an upward revision of the deficit target. In my view, this was the right approach. It did not make sense to insist on substantial further fiscal tightening to stay within the original target allowed for the fiscal deficit in the face of a weaker-than-projected economy, provided that the confidence of Argentina's creditors was reasonably well maintained.

Unfortunately, however, the Fund's flexibility in allowing an upward revision of the fiscal deficit target in the face of a weaker-than-expected economy was not applied symmetrically. Starting in late 1995, the Argentine economy began three years of very rapid recovery, significantly more rapid than was assumed in setting the (nominal) fiscal targets for the Fund-supported programs in this period. Normally, one should have expected that the Argentine government's fiscal deficit would have come in well below the permitted target—which, as always in Fund programs, was clearly defined as a ceiling for the fiscal deficit that was not to be exceeded and not as an objective to be hit exactly.

However, the deficit never came in well below the target; generally it was just below or even slightly above the permitted limit. Indeed, during the period from 1995 through 1998, the deficit of the Argentine government was within the quarterly limits prescribed at the beginning of each year under the IMF-supported program less than half of the time. More than half of the time, waivers were granted for missed fiscal performance criteria, or these criteria were met but only after they had been revised upward, or the violations (at the ends of some years) were simply ignored by the Fund and effectively swept under the rug. During 1995, when the recession turned out to be steeper than assumed at the start of the Fund-supported program, there was plausible reason to grant waivers and make upward adjustments to the deficit limits, rather than to try to force sharp additional fiscal tightening to meet the originally prescribed program targets.

At other times, however, when the Argentine economy was generally growing strongly, it is difficult to understand why the Fund did not make active use of its conditionality to press the Argentine government to maintain a more responsible fiscal policy. Rather, to avoid embarrassing the Argentine authorities, the Fund placed little emphasis on Argentina's transgressions of the initially specified fiscal targets, especially in public. And the fiscal targets were significantly less demanding than they appeared to be (even allowing for stronger-than-expected economic growth), because they conveniently ignored substantial amounts of government borrowing that were viewed by the Argentines as off budget.

All of this was quite different from what happens when the Fund wants to make a point and to press a program country to strengthen its policies and, as a consequence, there are delays in completing program reviews and in concluding negotiations for new programs or the later phases of established programs. In sum, the failure of the Argentine government to maintain a sufficiently prudent fiscal policy that effectively restrained the increase in public debt when the Argentine economy was performing well was surely a key—indeed, arguably, the key—*avoidable* policy problem that ultimately contributed to the tragic collapse of Argentina's stabilization and reform efforts. The Fund's tepid efforts to press the Argentine government to maintain a more responsible fiscal policy appear to be more a part of this problem than a part of its solution.

In mitigation, it should be noted that after successfully navigating the strains of the tequila crisis, Argentina was widely seen as one of the most successful emerging-market economies. Its economic policies were widely praised in the official international community. Indeed, as a hero of successful economic stabilization and reform, President Menem was accorded the unique honor of appearing jointly with US President Bill Clinton to address the IMF-World Bank Annual Meetings in Washington in October 1998. Private financial markets roared their approval as well by financing large amounts of Argentine borrowing at attractive spreads relative to most other emerging-market debtors, with the Emerging Markets Bond Index Plus spread for Argentina typically running well below the average spread for all emerging-market borrowers from 1997 through 1999.

These favorable assessments reflected the important successes that had been achieved by Argentina's stabilization and reform efforts in the 1990s, after many decades of dismal policies and performance. Indeed, with the collapse into financial crisis of many previously successful Asian emerging-market economies in 1997–98 and the developing difficulties in Brazil and Russia, Argentina stood out as one clear success story. With the Fund under widespread criticism (rightly or wrongly) for its involvement in Asia, it was particularly gratifying to be able to point to at least one important program country where the Fund appeared to be supporting successful economic policies. In this situation, there was probably even more than the usual reluctance for the Fund to be the skunk at the garden party by stressing the accumulating failures of Argentine fiscal policy.

Convertibility and Bust

The Convertibility Plan adopted in early 1991 played a central role both in the success of Argentina's stabilization and reform efforts during the past decade and in their ultimate tragic collapse. The essential objective of the plan was to end decades of financial and economic instability by ensuring that Argentina would have sound money. This was to be accomplished by linking the value of the domestic currency at parity to the US dollar, with the guarantee that pesos could be exchanged for dollars at will. The Argentine central bank was given independence from the government, under the mandate that it maintain convertibility by holding dollar reserves against its domestic monetary liabilities (currency and commercial bank reserves).

This 100 percent reserve requirement could be relaxed to 80 percent in emergency situations declared by the government, and the central bank could then hold up to 20 percent of its assets in government debt. Otherwise, the central bank was prohibited from printing money to finance the government. These features were meant to provide credible assurance that the persistent Argentine problem of rapid inflation generated by monetization of fiscal deficits could not be repeated under the Convertibility Plan.

Beyond the Convertibility Plan itself, the Argentine government undertook important measures to assure a sound banking system, especially after the tequila crisis. Commercial banks were privatized, and most of these banks were taken over by large foreign banks based in Spain and the United States. Commercial banks were required to be well capitalized and prudently managed; and, after 1995, they were encouraged to arrange foreign lines of credit that could be drawn in the event of a foreign exchange crisis. Commercial banks could do business in either dollars or pesos, but they generally maintained a reasonable balance between assets and liabilities denominated in the two currencies; the banks were further protected by the government's guarantee of convertibility of pesos into dollars. (The strength of the banks, however, would be seriously undermined if the government defaulted on the substantial volume of claims held by banks, or if the Convertibility Plan collapsed and led to defaults by Argentine borrowers on their dollar-denominated loans from banks.)

As is often the case with exchange-rate-based stabilization efforts, particularly from situations of hyperinflation, the Convertibility Plan performed very well initially. With the new peso rigidly pegged to the dollar, the inflation rate collapsed from 4,000 percent a year to single digits within three years. With reasonable assurance of monetary stability, the Argentine economy recovered rapidly from the economic devastation wrought by hyperinflation. As was noted above, however, the real exchange rate appreciated and the current account moved into a significant deficit; see figures 2.4 and 2.5. This was a pattern common in exchange-rate-based stabilizations, often leading to foreign exchange crises and the collapse of stabilization efforts. The Fund was rightly concerned that this problem might also engulf Argentina's Convertibility Plan.

The crucial test of the Convertibility Plan came in the tequila crisis of 1995. Here, the strengths of the plan, in contrast to many efforts at exchange-rate-based stabilizations, made themselves apparent. The government used the emergency provisions to relax the constraint of 100 percent foreign-currency reserves, and this allowed the Central Bank of Argentina some room to avoid as tight a monetary policy as would otherwise have been forced by the loss of reserves. Nevertheless, monetary conditions were tightened considerably and interest rates rose to substantial premiums over corresponding US rates.

Commercial banks came under significant pressure as high interest rates and a weakening economy undermined credit quality, and deposits flowed out of the banking system because of fears of bank failures or possibly of a break in the exchange rate peg. A few small banks did fail, but the banking system as a whole, notably all the large banks, survived the pressures of the crisis—crucial evidence of both the importance and the success of the measures that had been undertaken to strengthen the banking system.

In addition, Argentina had good luck externally: the US dollar depreciated sharply in early 1995, improving Argentine competitiveness in European markets; the Brazilian real strengthened markedly, improving Argentine competitiveness relative to that key trading partner; and interest rates in US capital markets fell back as it became clear that policy tightening by the US Federal Reserve was at an end and a shift toward easing (which began in the summer of 1995) might be in store. Were it not for the substantial improvements in bank soundness and for the external good luck, the Convertibility Plan might not have survived the tequila crisis.

After the test of the tequila crisis was successfully passed, some might argue that the time was ripe for an orderly exit from the Convertibility Plan. The main benefits of an exchange-rate-based stabilization had already been achieved, and many of the foundations for monetary stabil-

Figure 2.4 Real effective exchange rate, Argentina, 1980–2001

index: 1993 = 100

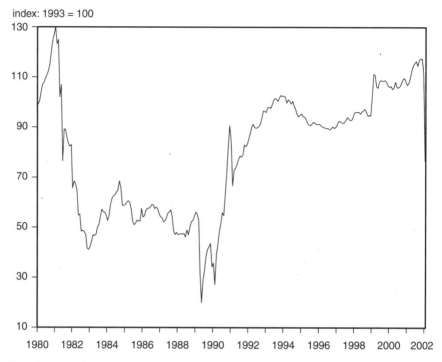

Note: The real effective exchange rate index is based on the consumer price index.

ity without an exchange rate peg had been put in place. Argentina was surely not part of an optimum currency area with the United States, because the Argentine economy was subject to much different shocks from the US economy and the monetary policy appropriate for Argentina need not generally coincide with that appropriate for the United States. Moreover, by this stage, Brazil was Argentina's largest trading partner, and a potential collapse of Brazil's exchange-rate-based stabilization effort was an important risk for Argentina and its Convertibility Plan. Clearly, looking back with the knowledge of recent developments, one would have to say that an earlier, more orderly exit from the Convertibility Plan would have been preferable to the present tragedy.

On the other hand, there were sound reasons for the Fund to continue to support the Convertibility Plan in the years after the tequila crisis. The Argentine government was determined to preserve the plan (or possibly even consider a move to full dollarization), and the plan undoubtedly enjoyed wide and deep popular support in Argentina. After enduring decades of financial instability, punctuated by occasional financial crises, most Argentines were particularly appreciative of the stability that had

Figure 2.5 Argentina's current account balance, 1980–2001

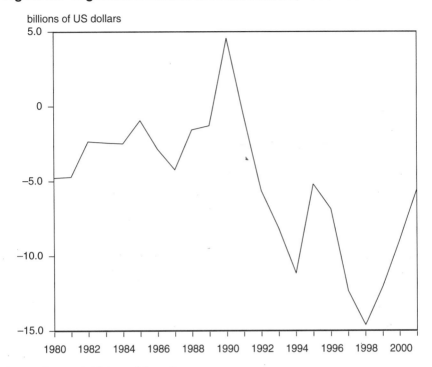

billions of US dollars

Source: Economic Ministry of Argentina.

been produced by the plan. Some, of course, recognized that the constraints imposed by the plan had important costs. In the tequila crisis, unemployment rates rose substantially, and they remained relatively high in the subsequent recovery. There was great pressure to bring down domestic costs, particularly in industries exposed to external competition; and this resulted in downward adjustments in nominal and real wages. Workers in the affected industries, many labor union leaders, and some politicians (especially Peronists) were not happy. However, to the extent that Argentines more generally were concerned with these problems, they did not necessarily attribute them to the Convertibility Plan; and, in any event, they were not inclined to abandon the plan with the risk that implied to financial stability and to the value of their own savings.

Indeed, among the supporters of the Convertibility Plan, there were those who saw that one of its important benefits was to force painful but necessary changes on the Argentine economy and society. After decades of protectionism and other government interventions to support specially favored sectors of the economy, the institutions of Argentine labor markets needed to become more flexible and the Argentine economy needed to become more efficient. From this perspective, the Convertibility Plan, which enjoyed broad and deep political support, provided the political leverage to achieve these desirable results.

At the Fund, sympathies undoubtedly lay with those who wanted to reform the Argentine economy in directions that would better allow it to reach its full productive potential. And the Argentine authorities who wished to preserve the Convertibility Plan appeared to be inclined in this direction. This, however, is not what induced the Fund to support the Argentine authorities in their decision to attempt to preserve the plan. Rather, in keeping with its Articles of Agreement (especially Article IV, Section 2), the Fund was required to support the basic policy strategy chosen by the duly constituted authorities of Argentina, as long as that strategy had at least a reasonable chance of success.

Until quite recently, perhaps as late as mid-2001, it was not clear that the Convertibility Plan was doomed to collapse in a catastrophic crisis. If sufficiently forceful measures had been undertaken early enough (particularly to reduce the fiscal deficit), the difficulties of the Argentine economy during the period 1999–2001 would not have been entirely avoided, but the outcome of the present crisis could have been much more favorable under plausible alternative scenarios that included preservation of the plan.

One might argue that Argentina would be better off in the long run without the Convertibility Plan than under this plausible alternative scenario. But the fundamental choice of Argentina's monetary policy framework and exchange rate regime was a choice for the duly constituted government of Argentina. The Fund could advise on the relative merits of different policy regimes and their relevance to Argentina. However, under the principles that govern the behavior of the International Monetary Fund as a voluntary association of sovereign members, the basic choice of regime is a decision of the member—at least up to the point where the chosen regime has no reasonable chance of success under policies that could plausibly be implemented.

Thus, though an independent observer might reasonably conclude that the rigidities of the Convertibility Plan deserve relatively more weight, and the failures of Argentine fiscal policy correspondingly less weight, in the blame for the tragedy that ultimately befell Argentina, this is not the relevant perspective from which to view the role of the Fund. For the Fund, the relevant question was—given the choice of Argentina to adopt and maintain the Convertibility Plan—what other policies were necessary to make the stabilization and reform effort a success. Given the plan, failure to maintain a sufficiently prudent fiscal policy would likely prove a fatal error. The Fund, having accepted the Convertibility Plan, had the responsibility to press very hard to avoid this fatal error.

3

Down the Road to Catastrophe

It is difficult to know at what point an economic catastrophe for Argentina became inevitable. The collapse of Brazil's exchange-rate-based stabilization effort, the Real Plan, in early 1999 was an important negative shock for Argentina. This was well understood in global financial markets, and interest rate spreads on Argentine bonds rose along with (although not as much as) Brazilian spreads as doubts about the sustainability of the Real Plan deepened in the autumn of 1998 and early 1999. When the collapse came in mid-January 1999 and intense financial turmoil continued in Brazil for another month, the spillover effects effectively shut Argentina out of global financial markets. However, as the situation in Brazil calmed down during the spring of 1999 (with the aid of exceptionally adept management of Brazilian monetary policy by the new central bank governor), Argentina regained access to global credit markets, and usually on relatively attractive terms.

The success of Argentina in floating substantial amounts of sovereign debt in global credit markets during much of 1999 and the first half of 2000 testifies both to the special conditions in those markets and to Argentine authorities' particularly deft management of the public debt. With the advent of the euro (and in anticipation of that event), interest rates for previous high-yield borrowers within the euro area converged downward toward the yields of the lowest-rate borrowers. This left a clientele of investors in the euro area with potential interest in higher-yielding instruments. Argentina was quick to exploit this market opportunity with issues denominated in the new multilateral currency.

The Argentine debt managers were also careful to avoid excessive reliance on short-term debt or on instruments with floating interest rates.

Such borrowing often has somewhat lower costs than financing through medium- and longer-term fixed-rate instruments, but it is much more dangerous for a country like Argentina that may be under sudden pressure to raise short-term rates in the face of pressures on the exchange rate or doubts about fiscal sustainability. Financial markets undoubtedly respected and probably rewarded Argentina's prudent debt management policies.

Argentine debt management also benefited from a good domestic market for Argentine government debt. Confidence in the Convertibility Plan and in the measures to ensure a sound banking system clearly contributed to a massive reflation of domestic credit. Because domestic financial institutions are important holders of sovereign debt, this credit reflation created an important domestic market for government debt. In addition, the reforms adopted by the Argentine government included the creation of funded pension plans. The assets accumulated by these plans were substantial, and a significant fraction of these assets consisted of investments in Argentine government debt. The existence of a substantial, relatively stable domestic market for Argentine government debt was also presumably reassuring to international investors and, accordingly, tended to support their demand for Argentine instruments.

On the policy front, developments during 1999 and the first half of 2000 were less reassuring than those on the financial front. President Menem's quest for a constitutional amendment that would permit him to run for a third consecutive term was clearly not a spur to determined efforts at fiscal consolidation, from the start of his second term in 1995 through much of his final year in office (which ended in December 1999). And after this possibility was finally laid to rest, election-year concerns further depressed the normally low level of interest that most Argentine politicians, at all levels of government, attached to measures of fiscal prudence. Meanwhile, the continuing recession in the Argentine economy (which began in late 1998) was depressing tax revenues and increasing demands for compensatory social spending—thus contributing to an already difficult environment for efforts to rein in the fiscal deficit.

Conditions deteriorated during the second half of 2000 as the recession continued and as turmoil within the administration of President Fernando de la Rua (including the resignation of the vice president) both inhibited decisive action and undermined confidence. Analysts of the Argentine economy—who (with some exceptions) had remained supportive of the longer-run viability of the government's finances through 1999—began to turn pessimistic, and the possibility of a default on Argentina's sovereign debt was openly discussed.

At the International Monetary Fund as well, concerns mounted about the deteriorating situation in Argentina as the recession deepened and the fiscal deficit continued to grow. By October, it appeared that the (not overly ambitious) fiscal deficit target in the Fund-supported program for the end of 2000 might well be missed. Even if this embarrassment could somehow be avoided (or swept under the rug, as on two earlier occasions), it was clear that the Argentine government would face severe difficulties in meeting its financing requirements for 2001; the possibility of sovereign default loomed.

Because the sovereign debt of Argentina was mainly fixed rate and medium term, it did not face the challenge of rolling over large amounts of short-term debt or the threat that the budgetary effect of an upward spike in interest rates would suddenly make the fiscal situation unsustainable. However, with little prospect of generating substantial primary surpluses that would pay off much of the debt as it matured, the Argentine government did face a large continuing need to refinance its large debt. For each of the five years from 2001 through 2005, projected financing requirements were about $22 billion—under the (optimistic) assumption that the fiscal deficit could be contained to a level that roughly stabilized the ratio of debt to GDP. Domestic sources might reasonably be expected to supply about half of the needed financing: through continuing rollover of a modest amount of short-term domestic-currency debt; and through the rollover of (and some additional investment in) medium- and longer-term dollar-denominated debt by domestic holders, notably banks and pension funds. The remainder of the needed financing would need to come from external sources.

By late 2000, the Argentine government was the largest emerging-market borrower on international credit markets, with outstanding obligations amounting to slightly more than 20 percent of the entire asset class. Shrewd debt management and careful exploitation of all available market opportunities had enabled the Argentine sovereign to float substantial new debt issues on international markets in 1999 and 2000. But the market was becoming saturated. With rising doubts about Argentina's ultimate ability and willingness to service its debts, the government needed to demonstrate its capacity to restrain its appetite for public borrowing to within reasonable limits before international credit markets would willingly take on additional exposure—or even agree to roll over most of their maturing claims.

Options for the Fund and the International Community

For the Fund, the deteriorating situation in Argentina in the autumn of 2000 presented a critical challenge. An important emerging-market country was already in deep economic difficulty and was potentially on the threshold of sovereign default and financial chaos. A star pupil that the Fund had praised and supported as a model of economic stabilization and reform was in danger of turning into a basket case.

By November, Argentina appeared likely to breach the revised fiscal performance criteria for the end of 2000 (which the Fund had already agreed in September to change to accommodate a larger deficit). This could have provided a plausible excuse for the Fund to announce a suspension of its financial support for Argentina in late 2000—as had been done with a number of countries whose Fund-supported programs had gone persistently off track. However, the failures of Argentina to achieve the agreed-on fiscal objectives of its Fund-supported program in 2000 (as in 1999) were to a considerable extent attributable to the economy's weaker-than-expected performance.

For a country of the importance of Argentina that was making some constructive efforts to address its policy deficiencies, it would have been unusual—but not unprecedented—for the Fund to announce publicly a suspension of its support. However, unlike many countries where the Fund had announced interruptions in its financial support, Argentina appeared to be particularly vulnerable to potentially catastrophic consequences. Announcement of a suspension of Fund support might well provoke a financial crisis that would lead to sovereign default, a collapse of the Convertibility Plan, and financial and economic chaos. The Fund (and the international community more broadly) needed at least to consider other options.

One approach would have been to continue with an essentially standard Fund-supported program. Levels of official financial support would be within the normal boundaries for such programs; that is, up to 100 percent of its Fund quota (about $3 billion) plus additional moderate amounts from the World Bank and the Inter-American Development Bank. The policies under the program would involve preservation of the Convertibility Plan and would emphasize efforts at fiscal consolidation to contain public borrowing needs, reassure private creditors, and maintain market access.

The main difficulty with this approach was that, by late 2000, it seemed very unlikely to succeed because participants in international financial markets would see that it was clearly inadequate. Under this approach, Argentina would need to access international credit markets for substantial amounts of financing during 2001, even if it succeeded in achieving the fiscal objectives in a tough adjustment program. With financial markets skeptical about Argentina's medium- and longer-term fiscal sustainability, if such large-scale private financing were available at all, it would probably only be on terms so onerous that they would confirm market fears about fiscal sustainability. The likely outcome would be that Argentina would be forced into sovereign default and probable collapse of the Convertibility Plan some time in the first part of 2001. Thus, this approach appeared to be a polite way for the official community to abandon Argentina without explicitly saying so.

A second approach would have been to conclude that because of the continuing recession and the lack of political support, there was no realistic hope that the Argentine government could implement a fiscal policy that would avoid a messy sovereign default. Further official support for Argentina, within reasonable limits for such support, would not be adequate to avoid default. Instead, Argentine authorities should be advised that further official support would be available only on the condition that Argentina reach agreement with its private creditors that would substantially reduce its financing requirements in coming years—to an extent that would provide credible assurance that official support advanced by the Fund and other agencies would be repaid in a timely manner.

Necessarily, this rescheduling of private credits could not be entirely voluntary, because private creditors would be required to accept significant modifications of their existing claims that would reduce their market values. On the other hand, private creditors would benefit from the likelihood of a more favorable long-run outcome made possible by the continuation of official support (contingent on write-downs of private credits) and by the conditionality applied to the behavior of the Argentine authorities.

The main argument in favor of this second approach was that by late 2000 it was already likely that, sooner or later, Argentina would need to restructure its outstanding private credits in a less than fully voluntary manner. The alternative course, relying on further fiscal tightening to contain government borrowing and regain market confidence, might succeed; but the likelihood of such success was limited. Accordingly, it would be better to accept the damage likely to accompany any involuntary restructuring at a time when Argentina still had ample reserves—as well as additional support from the Fund and the official community—that could be used to help contain the damage from such a restructuring. In particular, if debt restructuring were pursued at this stage, there was at least some hope that the Convertibility Plan could be preserved, or that the mess associated with its collapse could be managed somewhat better than has actually turned out to be the case.

Moreover, the second approach would have been consistent with the principles just enunciated by the Fund's International Monetary and Finance Committee at its ministerial meeting in Prague. Once it became clear that a country could not reasonably be expected to continue servicing its private credits on their contractual terms, the Fund would continue to provide financial support only on the condition that a country seek a reasonable understanding with its private creditors that would reduce debt-service requirements to sustainable levels.

On the other hand, it had to be recognized that any effort by Argentina to restructure its private credits in a nonvoluntary manner would be viewed as a de facto sovereign default and would likely be very messy. If, as was not unlikely, a significant number of creditors refused to participate and pursued legal actions for collection, the process of resolving these disputes could drag on for years, and Argentina would be precluded from access to international credit markets for a protracted period. Very likely, in the face of de facto sovereign default, the Convertibility Plan would become untenable. The government's credibility would be seriously damaged, including the credibility of its commitment to maintain the Convertibility Plan. This would probably lead to a run on domestic money and bank deposits, leading to sharp declines in limited foreign exchange reserves and to a severe contraction of domestic credit. The solvency of, and confidence in, the domestic banking system would also be seriously impaired by de facto sovereign default, both from the direct effect of reductions in the value of government securities held by banks and from the effects of deposit runs and credit contraction as Argentines fled from all domestic assets of questionable value (including dollar-denominated deposits in Argentine banks).

Thus, a decision by the Fund in late 2000 to press Argentina into a debt restructuring that would have amounted to a de facto sovereign default would have been a very weighty matter. The Argentine government was dead set against such action. Argentina's private creditors would have been outraged. And, while it could be argued by late 2000 that a restructuring of Argentina's sovereign debt might become unavoidable, the evidence of its necessity by that stage was not yet overwhelming. Nevertheless, some in the official community appeared to favor this approach, or something close to it. This included those who were deeply opposed to large packages of official financial support, those who were especially (in my view, excessively) concerned with the possible moral hazard effects of such packages, and those who strongly favored the substantial involvement (and punishment) of private creditors as an essential counterpart for official efforts to help resolve major international financial crises.

At the Fund, however, there was little enthusiasm for this approach. Some recognized that there was a significant risk of sovereign default, collapse of the Convertibility Plan, and financial chaos (while others merely shuddered at such possibilities). But in the autumn of 2000, the Argentine situation was not seen as without realistic hope of a better outcome—especially if Argentine policy could be put on a better path. Sovereign default is an exceptionally serious step that should only be taken as a last resort. Sovereign default is also properly the decision of the government involved; the Fund (and the international community) should not press for such a decision except when there is clearly no other viable alternative. Similarly, reneging on the Argentine government's solemn commitment to maintain the Convertibility Plan was not something that the Fund could reasonably advise (under the threat of suspension of Fund support) as long as there was a reasonable chance that the system could be preserved and the Argentine authorities desired to pursue that chance.

The third approach—the approach actually adopted—was to proceed with a Fund-supported program for Argentina for 2001 with levels of support substantially greater than in standard Fund-supported programs (to be achieved by a substantial augmentation of the substantial support already committed by the Fund under the existing three-year Stand-By Arrangement). As in the first approach, the policies under this program would emphasize fiscal consolidation, both in the deficit targets to be achieved for 2001 and in more fundamental measures (including better discipline on deficit spending by the provinces) to ensure fiscal sustainability in the longer term.

Under the program, the deficit target would be set so as to carefully balance the need to keep borrowing within responsible limits and show credible actual progress in achieving essential fiscal discipline against the very real economic and political difficulties of fiscal consolidation in a deepening recession. Official financing would be sufficiently generous to meet virtually all of Argentina's projected external financing requirements for 2001, assuming that the program's fiscal objectives were met. Official financing would be available on a more limited basis to meet part of projected external financing needs for the subsequent two years. (The headline figure for financial support associated with the program was almost $40 billion, with about $14 billion from the Fund, $5 billion from the Inter-American Development Bank and the World Bank, and $1 billion from the government of Spain. According to the Fund, the package also included ". . . about $20 billion of financing from the private sector that relies on a market-based, voluntary approach intended to complement Argentina's objective of assessing international capital markets as soon as confidence returns" [Fund Press Release 01/3, 12 January 2001]. This money, however, was not effectively committed to support Argentina; it was likely to come only if the program succeeded.)

The objective of this third approach was to give Argentina one last chance to avoid the catastrophe likely to ensue from sovereign default and a probable collapse of the Convertibility Plan. Success was not assured even if the Argentine government lived up fully to its policy commitments; success was highly doubtful if there was any substantial policy failure, especially in the critical fiscal area. But the international community, led by the Fund, at least was pledging a level of financial support that offered a further window of opportunity to demonstrate a willingness and ability to pursue the difficult measures necessary to attain fiscal sustainability. Also, the international community would be sending an important signal by pledging support to Argentina on a scale similar to that of other important countries that had faced severe international financial crises in recent years; whereas significantly less generous support for Argentina would likely be seen as quite a negative signal.

Moreover, from the perspective of the Fund, a substantial support package for Argentina could be seen as consistent with the general principle of "uniformity of treatment," which is one of the basic tenets that is supposed to govern all of the Fund's activities. Unless Argentina was, for some substantive reason, significantly less deserving than other members that had received large support packages or could reasonably be judged to be significantly less likely to succeed in its stabilization efforts, the principle of uniformity of treatment argued that Argentina should be given a last chance to avoid catastrophe—with a level of international support (subject to appropriate conditionality) consistent with that made available in other roughly similar cases.

In retrospect, because the Argentine case has ended in sovereign default and a messy collapse of the Convertibility Plan, one might reasonably argue that an earlier move toward this alternative would have done no harm and might have done some good. The latter would be the case if the resources from the international community used to attempt to avoid the collapse were instead conserved to help deal with its consequences, or if the collapse would have been better managed if undertaken in an earlier, better-planned manner. Indeed, I shall argue below that one of the important costs of the (in my view, misguided) decision to augment Fund support for Argentina in the summer of 2001 was precisely that this support was wasted on what was already clearly a lost cause. Was this not also the case with the decision in December 2000 that initiated Fund support for Argentina on an exceptional scale? Was not that key decision also a serious mistake?

The answer depends primarily on the assessment, in late 2000, of whether Argentina still had a realistic chance of avoiding de facto sovereign default and a likely collapse of the Convertibility Plan—which would surely have very dire consequences, including a potential collapse of the financial system—and whether the Argentine authorities were prepared to pursue policies that offered reasonable hope of realizing that chance. Indeed, after extended deliberations in official bodies (and probably with Argentina partly in mind), the Fund's International Monetary and Finance Committee set forth, in the communiqué of its 24 September 2000 ministerial meeting in Prague, the options to be considered and the considerations to be weighed in situations where a country faced a possible disruption in its payments to private creditors:

> The Committee agrees that the operational framework for private sector involvement must rely as much as possible on market-oriented solutions and voluntary approaches. The approach adopted by the international community should be based on the IMF's assessment of a country's underlying payment capacity and prospects for regaining market access. In some cases, the combination of catalytic official financing and policy adjustment should allow the country to regain full market access quickly. *The Committee agrees that reliance on the catalytic approach at high levels of access presumes substantial justification, both in terms of its likely effectiveness and of the risks of alternative approaches.* In other cases, emphasis should be placed on encouraging voluntary approaches, as needed, to overcome creditor coordination problems. *In yet other cases, the early restoration of full market access may be judged to be unrealistic, and a broader spectrum of actions by private creditors, including comprehensive debt restructuring, may be warranted to provide for an adequately financed program and a viable medium-term payments profile. This includes the possibility*

that, in certain extreme cases, a temporary payments suspension or standstill may be unavoidable. [emphasis added]

Stripping out the bureaucratic mumbo jumbo, a decision to commit large-scale assistance from the Fund should depend on the likelihood of a program's success and the likely consequences if the program failed and the country was forced into a de facto default and restructuring of its debts to private creditors. Though skeptical that the chance of success was as great as 50 percent, my view was (and is) that in late 2000 there still was a reasonable chance that what would otherwise be an economic and financial disaster of great magnitude could be avoided—if the Argentine government assiduously implemented fiscal measures that reassured private creditors about longer-term debt sustainability.[1]

Evidence supporting this assessment included the fact that Argentina still had ample international reserves, with a significant margin above the size of the domestic monetary base. Indeed, the loss of reserves that Argentina sustained between late summer and mid-November 2000 was recovered as negotiations on a new Fund-supported program progressed. Also, despite a modest downturn from October to December, deposits in Argentine banks remained near their peak level and, in light of the weak economy, signs of stress in the banking system were quite limited. There had been no major runs on Argentine banks or other clear signs of a domestic collapse of confidence in the sustainability of the Convertibility Plan or in the solvency of the government. Externally, there was the hope in late 2000 that the evident slowdown in the US economy might lead to both an easing of monetary policy in the United States and a downward correction of the US dollar against the euro, each of which would help Argentina (as had happened in the tequila crisis in 1995).

In international capital markets in late 2000, interest rate spreads on Argentine sovereign debt had risen to about 750 basis points above US Treasuries, up from about 550 basis points a year earlier; see figure 3.1. And interest rate spreads on Argentine bonds in late 2000 had risen modestly and briefly above the average spread for emerging-market borrowers. This indicated rising concern about fiscal sustainability in Argentina, but not yet firm conviction that sovereign default was virtually inevitable. In fact, Argentina had survived the Brazilian crisis of late 1998 and early 1999 when spreads on Argentine sovereign debt had briefly breached 1,000 basis points and subsequently rose briefly to 800 basis points on two occasions, before falling back to more moderate levels.

---

1. Contrary to normal practice and protocol in the Fund, I was not kept informed about discussions with the Argentine authorities in November and December 2000 and was not consulted by Fund management in advance of its decision to recommend a large assistance package for Argentina. Accordingly, the view that I now take of that operation is not influenced by the position that I took in my official capacity at the time.

Figure 3.1 Interest rate spreads on Argentine sovereign debt and the Emerging Markets Bond Index

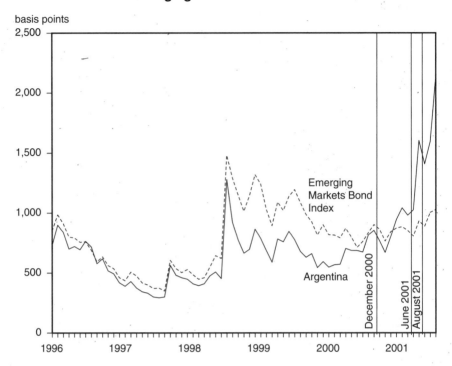

Note: End-of-month values.

Source: Economic Ministry of Argentina.

Indeed, relatively straightforward calculations indicate that at interest rate spreads of 500 to 600 basis points, Argentina's debt dynamics could have been sustainable under achievable degrees of budget discipline; whereas at persistent interest rate spreads of 1,000 basis points or more, the situation would be virtually hopeless. Formally, the condition of fiscal sustainability—that the ratio of pubic debt to GDP should not be rising persistently—may be stated as the condition that the ratio of the primary budget surplus to GDP, b, must be greater than or equal to the ratio of debt to GDP, d, multiplied by the difference between the interest rate on government debt, r, and the growth rate of the economy, g; that is, b must be greater than or equal to d times r minus g.

For Argentina in 2000–01, the ratio of public debt to GDP was about 50 percent, and for reasons discussed above, persistent increases above this ratio were not sustainable. Interest rates on medium-term US Treasuries in late 2000 were running around 5.5 percent, implying that with a spread of 550 basis points above US Treasuries, r would be about 11 percent. At this level of interest rates, prior experience suggests that the Argentine economy would probably be able to grow at a moderate pace, with little or no price inflation—say a growth rate of nominal GDP, g, of 4 percent a year. All of this suggests that a primary budget surplus, b, of about 3.5 percent (equal to 50 percent times the difference between 11 percent and 4 percent) would have been required for fiscal sustainability. A primary fiscal surplus of 3.5 percent of GDP would have been ambitious in an Argentine economy mired in deep recession. However, a successful effort to produce a consolidated budget surplus of 2 percent of GDP in the midst of recession might have established market confidence about what would be achieved in more normal economic circumstances.

In contrast, at interest rate spreads of 1,000 basis points above US Treasuries, r would have been at least 15 percent. At this level of interest rates, it would have been difficult for the Argentine economy to achieve much real growth, and deflation probably would continue at a modest pace. This suggests that g, the growth rate of Argentine nominal GDP, would have been about zero. Under these conditions, the primary budget surplus, b, would have to be at least 7.5 percent of GDP (equal to 50 percent times 15 percent minus zero) to achieve fiscal sustainability. It is inconceivable economically, and especially politically, that Argentina could have achieved a primary budget surplus of near this magnitude; and the economic effect of attempting to do so would likely have deepened the recession. Thus, sustained interest rate spreads above 1,000 basis points would be a clear signal that Argentina was headed for sovereign default.

With interest rate spreads rising to 750 basis points in late 2000, there was an urgent need for action to persuade financial markets that the Argentine government would find its way out of its fiscal difficulties and thereby induce a reduction in interest rate spreads to a level more plausibly consistent with fiscal sustainability and economic growth. But the situation did not appear hopeless. With determined action by the Argentine authorities and a pledge of substantial support from the Fund and the international community, there was still a realistic chance of success. However, if these efforts faltered or failed and interest rate spreads rose significantly, this would signal an irreparable loss of market confidence, and the game would almost surely end in tragedy.

Two other approaches to Argentina's difficulties might also have been considered in the autumn of 2000. President Menem and some in his administration had mused about moving from the Convertibility Plan to full dollarization—that is, replacing the peso completely with the US dollar. However, President de la Rua and his administration did not favor this approach. Even if moving to dollarization had been feasible and potentially desirable, it would have been inappropriate for the Fund to press a sovereign member for such a fundamental change in its monetary regime.

Another approach would have been a very big bailout that would have provided the Argentine government with guarantees of official support sufficient to cover its prospective financing requirements for several years, with repayment spread out many years into the future. However, this would have meant a substantial escalation in the magnitude and duration of official financing packages, and there was no support for this among the major countries that provide the Fund's resources. Indeed, following the controversies over previous large support packages, there was a consensus to move in the other direction: toward more modest amounts of official support and toward more consistent efforts to involve private creditors in the resolution of financial crises, including, when necessary, through involuntary sovereign debt restructurings.

Losing It

Argentina enjoyed a very brief period of respite in early 2001. On 3 January, Argentina got a boost as the US Federal Reserve cut US short-term interest rates and signaled the likelihood of further cuts. On 12 January, the Fund's Executive Board formally approved the augmentation of the Fund's Stand-By Arrangement for Argentina and authorized immediate disbursement of about $3 billion. Aided by these developments, spreads on Argentine sovereign debt fell to about 650 basis points, and the Argentine authorities took advantage of renewed access to international credit markets to float a large eurobond issue.

Unfortunately, however, Argentina's respite was short-lived. Political turmoil in Turkey helped to undermine confidence in that country's efforts to defend its crawling-peg exchange rate, which collapsed in a messy crisis in February; and contagion from this crisis was reflected in an increase in spreads for the Argentine sovereign. More important for Argentina, things were not going well at home. Fiscal results for the Argentine government for the fourth quarter of 2000 would likely reveal failure to meet the fiscal targets for the end of 2000.

This failure might, once again, be swept under the rug. But with revenues coming in well below program assumptions (due partly to the recession and partly to deteriorating tax compliance) and expenditures not particularly well contained, by February, fiscal results for the first quarter of 2001 also appeared at risk of exceeding program targets; and this would be impossible for the Fund to ignore. The deteriorating fiscal situation led to renewed concerns about Argentina in financial markets and to a renewed widening of spreads. The likely need to adopt additional measures of fiscal tightening to meet program targets heightened political tensions with the Peronist opposition in the Argentine Congress, with provincial political leaders, and within the Argentine government.

With dissension in the Argentine cabinet focused on economy minister Luis Machinea, President de la Rua decided to make a change in the head of his economic team. Ricardo Lopez-Murphy—a well-known Argentine economist who had been educated at the University of Chicago—was selected as the new economy minister. Within days, he proposed new measures of fiscal consolidation, focused on sharp reductions in public spending, to address the Argentine government's deteriorating fiscal position. Argentine politicians of all parties and ranks were outraged, including most of Lopez-Murphy's fellow ministers. The president refused to back his new economy minister and sided with the vast majority of Argentine politicians.

In my view, this event marked the effective end to any realistic hope that the Argentine government would address its fiscal difficulties with sufficient resolve to avoid sovereign default and its attendant chaos. In February, interest rate spreads on Argentine sovereign credits rose to 850 basis points and generally fluctuated between this level and 1,050 basis points through the spring. At this level of spreads, there was little hope either that the Argentine economy could begin a sustained recovery or that the debt dynamics of the Argentine sovereign could be put on a sustainable path.

Moreover, it was becoming increasingly clear that resolution of Argentina's potentially unstable debt dynamics through fiscal tightening was neither politically feasible nor economically sensible. On the political side, fiscal tightening is particularly difficult when a country is already in deep recession, and especially so in the Argentine system where the provinces can easily undermine the central government's austerity efforts. On the economic side, fiscal tightening in the midst of a deep recession tends to forestall economic recovery, which is essential to put debt dynamics on a sustainable path. Recognition of these difficulties made financial markets particularly sensitive both to political difficulties in achieving fiscal austerity and to adverse news on the performance of the Argentine economy. Once financial markets became persuaded that Argentina had no viable way out of this predicament, fears of sovereign default would become self-fulfilling.

After the departure of Lopez-Murphy, President de la Rua next called on the legendary Domingo Cavallo, author of the Convertibility Plan and genuine hero of Argentina's stabilization and reform efforts in the early 1990s, to resume his old post of economy minister. With his characteristic energy, Minister Cavallo rapidly secured Parliamentary approval for wide (but not unlimited) powers of the president to enact economic measures by decree.

Cavallo—eschewing the Lopez-Murphy approach of fiscal consolidation through expenditure restraint—focused primarily on taxes. A financial transactions tax (initially at a 0.25 percent rate and later raised to 0.4 and then 0.6 percent) was introduced to raise significant additional revenue. Some other measures sought to raise revenue, whereas others sought to spur investment and growth at the expense of revenues. The overall intended effect was to raise revenues—not enough to reach the original deficit targets for the first quarter of 2001, but enough to suggest that an upwardly revised deficit target for the second quarter could be met and that the original deficit target for the end of 2001 could still be attained.

In evaluating these measures vis-à-vis the agreed-on objectives in the Fund-supported program, the Fund's decisions were governed by its long-standing policies and practices. It is not infrequent that Fund-supported programs go off track and fail to meet their previously agreed-on objectives (spelled out in Fund conditionality). When this happens, the Fund member is almost always allowed to propose corrective policies which, if they offer the reasonable expectation of returning performance to the original program objectives, lead to a Fund decision to continue scheduled disbursements under the program. This is what happened for Argentina. In view of the new fiscal measures, violation of the fiscal target for the first quarter of 2001 was waived and the disbursement for that quarter (after a short delay) was made. The fiscal deficit target for the second quarter was revised upward somewhat, whereas the original fiscal deficit target for the end of 2001 ($6.5 billion) was maintained.

Notably, the key issue of whether the Fund-supported program for Argentina still had any realistic chance of avoiding de facto default and a likely collapse of the Convertibility Plan was not seriously addressed at this time. (The IMF Staff Report on Argentina of 14 May 2001, publicly released as IMF Country Report 01/90, contains an analysis of Argentina's debt dynamics. This analysis is examined in appendix A.) This was consistent with Fund practices going back 50 years. By the decision made by Fund management in December 2000 and ratified by the Executive Board in early January 2001, the Fund was effectively committed to continue disbursements under the program for Argentina as long as the Argentine authorities were making reasonable efforts to meet their policy commitments under that program. By March 2001, financial markets had apparently concluded that these efforts no longer had much chance of success; and this conclusion would very likely prove to be a self-fulfilling prophecy. Nevertheless, the Fund could not reasonably back out of a commitment it had already made to support Argentina's efforts to avoid a disastrous financial and economic crisis.[2] Indeed, a signal from the Fund that it would not continue with the support it had already committed to Argentina, despite the government's efforts to repair their program, would very likely have provoked that crisis.

---

2. Discussions by the Fund's Executive Board of the principles and policies that govern Fund support for members, especially in the context of Stand-By Arrangements, go back to the early 1950s. The conclusions of these discussions (and their implementation in actual cases) constitute an essential part of the "law of the Fund" which exerts great influence on how the Fund operates. From the start of these discussions, it has been recognized that once the Fund has committed its support, members must be able to rely on that support, provided that they are meeting its agreed-upon conditions.

In the face of deteriorating market confidence during the spring of 2001, Minister Cavallo pursued numerous new initiatives. These initiatives were often announced without consulting in advance with the Fund or even with most of his own staff. His actions in three areas are particularly noteworthy. In mid-April, he suddenly announced a change in the Convertibility Plan. Rather than being pegged at parity to the US dollar, the peso would instead be pegged 50 percent to the dollar and 50 percent to the euro. Initially, the new exchange rate would apply only to international trade transactions (and not to capital flows or services), and it would be implemented by a system of taxes on imports and subsidies to exports to avoid creating a "multiple exchange rate practice" that violated Argentina's commitments under the Fund's Articles of Agreement. Because Argentina trades about as much with the euro area as with the United States, the economic rationale for this initiative is an arguable issue. However, the effect on confidence in financial markets of the announcement of a change in the Convertibility Plan was clearly quite negative—at a time when confidence in financial markets was of critical importance for Argentina.

A second Cavallo initiative of spring 2001 concerned the Argentine Central Bank and its governor, the widely respected Pedro Pou. Governor Pou was not a fan of Minister Cavallo's efforts to adjust the Convertibility Plan or his desires to reduce the liquidity reserves that banks were required to hold and thereby have the central bank pursue a more accommodative monetary policy by stretching the limits of what was allowed under the Convertibility Plan. Both issues were debatable as to their economic merits. But the decision on these issues was within the province of the independent central bank, and Governor Pou was well within his legitimate authority to determine the decision—subject to his interpretation of the requirements of the Convertibility Plan.

As an important guarantee of the effective independence of the central bank, its governor could be removed only for cause, not at the whim of the economy minister or even the president. Cause was conveniently found; Governor Pou was accused of serious misconduct by failing to prevent certain money-laundering transactions by some Argentine branches of foreign banks. Whatever the merits of this accusation, it achieved its desired effect in securing the removal of Governor Pou. However, the effective independence of the central bank was clearly compromised and confidence in financial markets was further undermined, dealing another blow to confidence both domestically and internationally.

The third, and perhaps most important, Cavallo initiative was the large swap of Argentine government debt that was carried out at the end of May. This swap was voluntary, at least from the perspective of external holders of Argentine sovereign debt; it was not carried out under the threat of default—although worries about possible default clearly depressed the market value of Argentine sovereign debt at this time. The effect of the swap was to exchange nearly $30 billion of the face value of existing Argentine sovereign debt (including about $8 billion held externally) for new sovereign obligations. Interest and principal payments due between 2001 and 2005 were substantially reduced by the swap, at the expense of substantially higher interest and principal payments due over the next 25 years.

The debt swap was characterized as an important success by the Argentine government and its financial advisers (who earned substantial fees). It was a success at least in the limited respect that a substantial volume of debt was offered for exchange both by Argentina's domestic and foreign creditors. Indeed, an upward move in interest rate spreads attributable to fears that the offered swap would be a market flop was at least briefly reversed when the volume of tendered securities proved larger than expected.

However, a proper analysis of the effects of the swap for Argentina cannot be based on whether its creditors found the terms of the swap sufficiently attractive to motivate them to tender. Rather, the swap was a good deal for Argentina only if the benefits from the reductions in debt service during the period 2001–05 outweighed the costs of the additional debt-service obligations in later years. This, of course, is not a simple arithmetic comparison. With positive interest rates, the net (undiscounted) cost of a swap that lengthens the average maturity of the debt (by about three years, in the case of the Argentine swap) will be positive even for a deal that is quite beneficial from an Argentine perspective. The issue is how high a price is being paid to achieve a given increase in the maturity of the debt.

At the time the swap was carried out, the interest rate spread of Argentine sovereign bonds over US Treasuries was between 900 and 1,000 basis points, corresponding to an interest rate on Argentine sovereign debt of between 15 and 16 percent. Because holders of Argentine debt already had the opportunity to trade in the market Argentine debt of lower maturities for debt of higher maturities at these interest rates, they surely would not voluntarily accept an officially sponsored swap at less attractive terms. Consistent with this fact, in the swap, the Argentine government achieved a reduction in its debt-service obligations between 2001 and 2005 of only about $12 billion, at the expense of additional debt-service obligations of about $66 billion in the years beyond 2005.

Not surprisingly, in view of the level of market interest rates, it takes a discount rate of more than 16 percent to make the present value of this swap break even from the Argentine government's (and citizen's) perspective. This is a very high discount rate to apply for a country that (under the assumption that the Convertibility Plan is maintained) is not likely to enjoy an annual growth rate of GDP (measured in US dollars) that consistently exceeds 7 percent.

Indeed, as was argued above, interest rates for the Argentine sovereign of 16 percent (interest rate spreads of above 1,000 basis points) were not consistent with positive growth of the Argentine economy or with debt sustainability. By pursuing and accepting a debt swap on such onerous terms, the Argentine government was effectively declaring that it shared the market's assessment that sovereign default was virtually inevitable. Thus, the debt swap on these terms is properly viewed as an act of desperation by a debtor that is prepared to promise almost anything in the long term for relatively modest debt-service relief in the near term.

The Fund issued a very brief public statement that "welcomed . . . the announcement by the Argentine government of the successful conclusion of the debt exchange offer . . ." In the circumstances, it could hardly have done otherwise. However, beyond this statement, the Fund staff made a broader effort to analyze the consequences of the debt swap in depth and reach conclusions concerning its costs and benefits for Argentina. Notably, in much of this effort there was a tendency to portray the debt swap in the best possible light for the Argentine authorities that had undertaken it, rather than to recognize the simple truth that modest short-term debt-service relief had been secured at very high cost in terms of long-term debt-service obligations. This was symptomatic of the general tendency in the Fund to try to see things in the best possible way from the perspective of the member and its authorities.

Chutzpah

After a brief respite following the introduction of new measures to improve the fiscal balance and agreement on a somewhat revised program with the Fund (and disbursement of the tranche of Fund support due for the first quarter), sharp upward pressures on interest rate spreads for Argentine paper reemerged in late June and July 2001. One worry was that tax revenues were coming in below forecasts, raising concerns that even the revised fiscal targets for the second quarter might not be met. Probably more important, large-scale withdrawals of deposits from Argentine banks, which had been halted and partially reversed in the spring, resumed in July as Argentines became increasingly concerned about a possible breakdown in the Convertibility Plan. Also, the Argentine government was running very short of cash—a fact that the general public may well have surmised from widespread reports of delays in government payments, including transfers to provincial governments. With deposit runs accelerating and interest rate spreads spiking to 1,500 basis points above US Treasuries, something needed to be done quickly, or the game was about to end.

Through leaks to the local press, the Argentine government circulated the story that the Fund would accelerate its normal schedule for (favorable) consideration of its disbursement of about $1.25 billion, on the basis of satisfactory performance through the end of the second quarter. More important, the Fund would augment this disbursement with an addition of about $8 billion. Financial markets reacted positively to this news, and the bank runs slowed. A little later on, Minister Cavallo announced that, in conjunction with the augmented Fund support, the Argentine government would pursue a more ambitious fiscal policy—with the objective of reducing the fiscal deficit to zero from then onward. However, announcement of a zero-deficit plan did not assure its approval or, even more important, any realistic chance of its successful implementation. With the Argentine economy already in deep recession and spiraling downward under the pressure of crushingly high interest rates, the massive additional fiscal tightening needed to achieve a zero deficit was neither politically acceptable nor economically sensible. By the summer of 2001, the Argentine government was clearly trapped with no viable avenue of escape.

Nevertheless, Cavallo pressed on with his initiative in classic Cavallo style. The suggested augmentation of Fund support was announced without consultations with the rest of the Argentine government. Even some key Cavallo aides were taken by surprise. There were no prior consultations with the Fund, nor any prior indication of support from the Fund for a substantial augmentation of its lending. Indeed, Cavallo's tactic was to force the Fund to augment its lending by creating a fait accompli. Financial markets and Argentine citizens reacted favorably to the announcement of augmented Fund support. If they were disappointed that this support was not forthcoming, the Fund (and the international community more broadly) would be responsible for the consequences.

For those not familiar with how the Fund normally operates, it may be difficult to understand how great a perversion of its policies and principles was perpetrated in this incident. The Fund is not an aid agency; it does not give money to countries to ease their economic and financial distress. The Fund lends money to countries in support of a well-defined set of economic policies, especially monetary, fiscal, and exchange rate policies. The objective of such lending is to assist the country in meeting its international payments obligations, while that country is undertaking policies that give credible assurance that payments imbalances will be corrected—in a manner that avoids, to the extent possible, damage to national and international prosperity. To merit Fund support, a critical requirement of any policy program is that it must provide reasonable assurance that the resources lent by the Fund will be repaid in a timely manner.

In recommending a Fund-supported program for approval by the Fund's Executive Board, the managing director certifies that he is confident that the policies promised by the national authorities in their Letter of Intent to the Fund will be responsibly implemented and that under these policies there is credible assurance that the Fund will be repaid. The amount of resources pledged by the Fund to support a member's policies and the phasing of their disbursement is determined by the managing director (as his recommendation for approval by the Executive Board) at the end of negotiations over the program, on the basis of his assessment of the country's financing need and of the strength of the country's policy program. It has never been acceptable for a country to decide by itself the size of support it will receive from the Fund and to seek to impose its wishes through the fait accompli of a public announcement.

The Fund's emergency assistance to Russia during the summer of 1998 is a case in point. The Fund had an ongoing program with Russia, within the standard limits of Fund financing. During the first half of 1998, Russia's financial situation deteriorated sharply as its current account went into deficit (due partly to weakening world oil prices) and interest rates on the government's domestic-currency debt escalated as creditors became increasingly worried about potential default. The policy performance of the Russian government under the Fund-supported program since early 1996 had been—to put it politely—less than entirely satisfactory, especially in controlling the fiscal deficit.

Nevertheless, Russia was clearly a very important case, and there were important reasons, perhaps more political that economic, to give its government a last chance to avoid the chaos likely to result from devaluation or default. The managing director of the Fund, Michel Camdessus, took the initiative. He proposed a large augmentation of the Fund's support for Russia (beyond normal access limits) and arranged with the Fund's leading members to activate the General Agreements to Borrow in order to supply the Fund with additional liquidity to underwrite the operation.

For its part, the Russian government was required to strengthen its policy program, especially in the fiscal area. Indeed, before the approval of the augmented program and disbursement of the initial tranche of augmented support (about $5.5 billion out of a total of about $15 billion), the Russian government was required to implement a number of prior actions, including passage of certain legislation by the Russian Duma. When the Duma refused to pass two key measures, the Fund's managing director cut back the size of the initial disbursement by about $800 million. Neither the Russian government nor many of its political supporters were pleased with this decision, and financial markets reacted negatively. But the managing director had the authority to set access to Fund resources (subject to later approval by the Executive Board), and he was determined to show that the Fund was serious about its conditionality in a situation where determined action by the authorities was absolutely essential to restore market confidence and to provide some hope for the success of the program.

For Argentina, the December 2000 support package (approved by the Executive Board in January 2001) involved a large augmentation to an already existing Fund-supported program, beyond the normal limits of access. Similar to the July 1998 package for Russia, this December 2000 package for Argentina was supposed to support a last chance to strengthen its policies and avoid a catastrophe. By the summer of 2001, that last-chance effort was clearly failing. Yet, at its own initiative, the Argentine government was insisting on substantial additional support for a second last chance—perhaps to be followed by more last chances down the road.

Not only was the procedure unusual; the outcome—a Fund disbursement of more than $6 billion (announced in August and formally approved in early September), with a pledge of $3 billion more to support an unspecified debt restructuring—was extraordinary both in its size and in the lack of any reasonable justification. The disbursement was the second largest in Fund history. About $1.25 billion was the amount due for Argentina upon successful completion of the review of its performance through the end of the second quarter. It was reported that Argentina met the quantitative criteria of the Fund-supported program—most important, keeping the fiscal deficit within the revised limit permitted for that quarter. But the target on the cash deficit was met with the aid of substantial payment arrears: tax rebates under the value-added tax and export incentive schemes were delayed; transfers due to the provinces were withheld; and payments for government wages, pensions, and health and welfare benefits were deferred.

Under the Fund's traditional three-monkeys approach to assessing a member's performance—hear no evil, see no evil, speak no evil—such transgressions would often be ignored. As with the disbursement in May, the long-standing Fund policy of continuing disbursements under an already agreed-on program (provided that the member is meeting the explicit requirements of Fund conditionality) might reasonably have justified proceeding with the already scheduled disbursement of about $1.25 billion.

On the other hand, the Fund's decision on disbursement of the scheduled tranche was supposed to be based on a "program review"—which, in addition to a narrow appraisal of the satisfaction of quantitative performance criteria for the end of the second quarter, generally called for a forward-looking assessment of whether the program was on track and likely to meet its objectives at least through the end of the program year. With the Argentine economy performing well below the economic assumptions of the program, with interest rate spreads at levels (about 1,500 basis points) that clearly implied deepening recession and continuing deflation, and with no realistic chance of actually implementing fiscal measures that would (in these economic circumstances) come close to achieving the year-end deficit limits, an honest forward-looking assessment would have concluded that the program was headed irreparably off track. Such an assessment, perhaps reinforced by some critical reference to the substantial payments arrears that were used to meet the formal performance criteria for the end of the second quarter, ought to have sufficed to overturn the usually strong presumption that the Fund would continue with scheduled disbursements under an already established program (subject to nominal compliance with the explicit performance criteria).

More important, a large augmentation of the program (the disburse-ment of an additional $5 billion and the pledge of $3 billion more to support debt restructuring) clearly called for a de novo assessment of the entire Argentine program—as was done at the time of the December 2000–January 2001 decision to augment substantially Fund support for Argentina. Was there a reasonable expectation that the Argentine authorities would be able to implement the policies to which they were committed under the program; and, if so, was there a reasonable expectation that the program would succeed, especially in the key requirement that Argentina would be able to repay the Fund in a timely manner?

Arguably, in December 2000, it had been possible to answer these critical questions in the affirmative. Interest rate spreads for the Argentine sovereign had risen sharply to about 750 basis points, up from about 550 basis points a year earlier. With the commitment of a new, large package of international support, with determined and credible actions of the Argentine authorities to contain this deficit within responsible limits, and with some good luck (such as a shift by the US Federal Reserve toward monetary easing), there was at least a reasonable chance that a disastrous default and likely collapse of the Convertibility Plan might be avoided. Financial market confidence in Argentina could improve, allowing renewed market access at significantly reduced interest rate spreads. With capital-market access restored and interest rates reduced, economic recovery could begin and fiscal sustainability could be achieved with a politically feasible degree of budgetary restraint. Indeed, as was noted above, in January 2001, after formal approval of the new international support package and a clear signal of a shift toward an easing of US Federal Reserve policy, Argentina appeared, at least briefly, to be moving along this desirable course.

By August 2001, however, prospects for a favorable outcome were pure fantasy. In contrast to the situation eight months earlier, successive runs on Argentine banks had reduced bank deposits by more than $10 billion; see figure 3.2. Argentina also had suffered substantial losses of foreign exchange reserves (especially abstracting from the inflows of reserves from disbursements of Fund support); see figure 3.3. Most important, interest rate spreads for the Argentine sovereign had risen persistently above 1,000 basis points and were generally fluctuating in the range of 1,300 to 1,600 basis points. This implied nominal interest rates for the Argentine sovereign (which generally set the lower bound for other Argentine credits) of 18 to 22 percent, with real interest rates even higher due to deflation.

Economic recovery was impossible in this situation; and nominal GDP would surely continue to contract even more rapidly than real GDP, implying significant increases in the ratio of debt to GDP even if, by some miracle, the government budget were brought into overall balance. The Argentine government's fiscal policy, with its increasing reliance on unsustainable payments arrears, clearly could not meet its targeted objec-

Figure 3.2 Total bank deposits in Argentina, 1996–2001

billions of US dollars

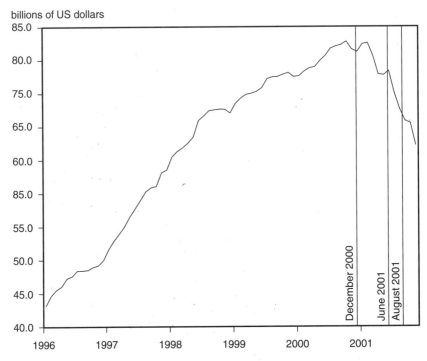

Source: Central Bank of Argentina.

tives. The political consensus to raise the huge primary surplus that would be required to demonstrate sustainable debt dynamics in these circumstances was, quite understandably, nowhere apparent and never likely to materialize. Substantial reserve losses had already occurred, and further bank runs were a continuing threat. An emergency injection of another $6 billion in cash from the Fund was urgently needed just to stave off immediate default and keep the farce going for another few months. If announcement of a large package of international support had helped to bring only brief respite in the relatively favorable circumstances of January, it was absurd to believe that a more modest augmentation of that package by another $5–8 billion would somehow produce a miracle in the clearly desperate circumstances of August. Looking at the facts, a wide range of analysts outside the Fund (and several at the Fund)—often with differing views on many issues—clearly concluded that the game was over for Argentina. Only a fool would conclude otherwise.

Why, then, did the Fund, and the international community more broadly, acquiesce in this folly? Both at the Fund and outside it, there was rightly a great deal of concern about the deteriorating situation in Ar-

Figure 3.3 Foreign exchange reserves in Argentina, 1996–2001

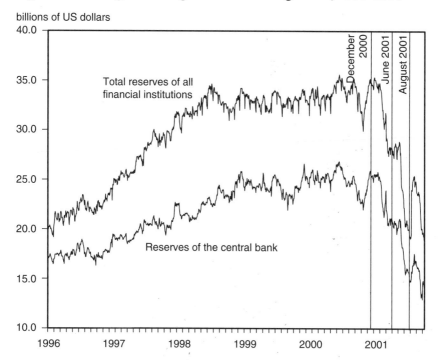

Source: Central Bank of Argentina.

gentina and about the disaster that would accompany a sovereign default and a likely simultaneous collapse of the Convertibility Plan and the Argentine financial system. Also, Argentina was generally seen as a country deserving of sympathy and support; and the Argentine authorities were certainly willing to draw on this sympathy and support. US President George Bush publicly expressed the concerns of his administration and its support for further assistance to Argentina. UK Prime Minister Tony Blair traveled to Argentina to emphasize similar views on the part of his country. German Chancellor Gerhard Schröder and the senior political leaders of many other European countries also voiced their concerns and support. And, beyond the genuine sympathy that was felt for Argentina, there was undoubtedly the desire, both inside and outside the Fund, to avoid the appearance of responsibility for Argentina's collapse.

In fact, however, the Fund's large September disbursement would do no more than postpone the catastrophe in Argentina by three months. This was known or should have been apparent to the top officials in the Fund and among the Fund's major members that together determined how the Fund would respond to Argentina's request for augmented support. Here there was a failure of intellectual courage—to face up to the realities of the situation in Argentina—and a failure of moral courage—to make the difficult decision to decline substantial additional support for policies that no longer had any reasonable chance of success.

Argentina was not helped. Indeed, external assistance that was potentially far more valuable in helping to contain the damage once a de facto sovereign default had occurred was instead squandered in a futile effort to avoid the inevitable. And a last opportunity to persuade the reluctant Argentine authorities to face very unpleasant realities and prepare for a potentially more orderly (although still difficult and dangerous) retreat was lost. Indeed, through the autumn of 2001 and until early December, the Fund maintained a dialogue with the Argentine authorities on the assumption that the measures needed to implement Cavallo's zero-deficit policy (including the cooperation of the provinces) might somehow be implemented and that Fund disbursements related to performance through the third quarter and the end of 2001 might be made (possibly with waivers or under somewhat revised performance criteria). Perseverance by the Fund in this charade clearly did not encourage the Argentine authorities to face up to the reality of their situation and to the painful but necessary decisions implied by this reality.

Damage was also done to the Fund and to its usefulness to the international community. Although much skepticism has been voiced in recent years, I believe that experience clearly demonstrates that there are important situations where large official support packages can be useful in containing the damage from international financial crises—without putting the public funds lent in such packages at substantial risk. This was so for Mexico in 1995, for South Korea in 1998, and for Brazil in 1999. (Thailand in 1997–98 is less clear, in my view; and Indonesia in 1997–98 and Russia in 1998 were clearly not successes.) However, even most advocates of the occasional use of large official support packages recognize that there must be limits, both on their size and on the circumstances where they are appropriate. Otherwise, problems of moral hazard could potentially become quite serious, and the official community could run the danger of assuming risks from private creditors that should not be transferred to the general public.

The Fund, and the power structure through which its decisions are made and approved, is the instrument through which the international community determines the conditions and circumstances in which large official support packages will, and will not, be provided. If the Fund fails to act (or not act) in a responsible manner—in accord with the principles and practices that, it is generally agreed, should govern its behavior—then the interests of the international community will not be properly served. In the end, if the Fund fails to do its job properly, its resources and its role as a valuable instrument of the international community will surely diminish. The Fund's performance in the case of Argentina during the summer and autumn of 2001 surely added to concerns in this regard.

Collapse

The late Herbert Stein was fond of observing that something which is unsustainable will not last. Even as the Fund's August augmentation was arriving (in early September 2001), the tragic end of Argentina's efforts to avoid default and preserve the Convertibility Plan was drawing near. Parliamentary and provincial elections in mid-October turned control of the national legislature and of most provincial governorships over to the opposition Peronists. That meant even less political support for austerity measures needed to implement Cavallo's zero-deficit policy at the central-government level. Negotiations with provincial governors for their necessary contribution to greater fiscal austerity bogged down. Tax revenues dwindled as economic activity continued to shrink and tax avoidance and evasion (always a favorite sport in Argentina) escalated, encouraged by the government's increasing dereliction of its own payments obligations. In world financial markets, the value of Argentine sovereign bonds plummeted further, with spreads over US Treasuries rising above 2,000 basis points.

Driven to the wall, Minister Cavallo announced that Argentina would have to approach its creditors to request a debt rescheduling that would substantially reduce debt-service requirements. The rescheduling was portrayed as entirely voluntary and market friendly, but clearly it would be neither. Domestic holders of Argentine government debt, primarily banks and pension funds, were approached first, and they were strong-armed into accepting new claims with lower interest rates and longer maturities. External creditors were told that they would be next, after the legal basis for the zero-deficit plan had been put in place. Debt service on external credits was maintained, however, to avoid a legally declared default.

By mid-November, the cash position of the government was again becoming precarious. Withdrawals of bank deposits and losses of foreign exchange reserves again began to accelerate. Minister Cavallo announced that he was prepared to travel to Washington to speak to the Fund about further disbursements. He was informed, rather chillily, by the Fund's new first deputy managing director that he would not be received. Learning from the debacle of August, world political leaders offered muted expressions of sympathy, but no suggestions of increased financial support. Chutzpah had worked once, but not twice. Nevertheless, a Fund mission continued to negotiate with the Argentine authorities over additional fiscal measures that might (if one believes in miracles) somehow make the zero-deficit objective seem achievable and justify continued Fund disbursements. Even at this late stage, the Fund apparently lacked the courage to tell the Argentine authorities forthrightly that the program was irredeemably off track and that very different and difficult policy alternatives needed to be considered.

In the last week of November, the run on Argentine banks escalated, reaching nearly $1 billion a day. With foreign exchange reserves down to $15 billion (barely enough to cover domestic currency in circulation), the end had come. The government was forced to close the banks and announce that when they reopened, cash withdrawals would be limited to $250 a week. This was described as a temporary measure, for up to three months; but Argentines generally realized the truth. The Convertibility Plan was finished. The banks were bust. Depositors would be lucky if they ultimately got anything near the book value of their claims. In the streets of Buenos Aires, pesos were exchanged for dollars at a discount of about 25 percent; across the Rio de la Plata in Montevideo, the discount was about 50 percent.

After more than three years of recession, with unemployment at nearly 20 percent and rising, deprived of access to their bank deposits, and with the value of the domestic currency rapidly depreciating in the black market, the Argentine people had finally had enough. Riots in the provinces spread to the capital. Stores were looted. Banks were ransacked. Foreign-owned businesses were attacked. In efforts to restore order, nearly 30 people died. Recognizing that his efforts had failed, Minister Cavallo resigned, and President de la Rua soon followed.

It is sad, most of all for Argentina, that a decade of stabilization and reform ended so tragically. It need not have been so. Even when sovereign default clearly became inevitable by the summer of 2001, a less catastrophic outcome might still have been managed. This would have required recognition of the need to seek a restructuring of Argentina's sovereign debt and a reasonable plan to deal with the consequences for the domestic financial system and for the viability of the Convertibility Plan. Prior consultation with the Fund and prearranged financial support to help contain the substantial disruption from debt restructuring and a likely break in the Convertibility Plan could have proved quite valuable—even though, with the best possible planning, management, and support, it still would have been a messy affair.

It is impossible to know at what point sovereign default and a likely collapse of the Convertibility Plan became unavoidable. Perhaps it was already too late by the autumn of 2000. But surely, the ultimate tragic collapse was not preordained from the time that Argentina's stabilization and reform efforts began a decade earlier. The Convertibility Plan clearly implied a very rigid framework for Argentina's exchange rate and monetary policy. This limited the options available to respond to adverse shocks, such as those associated with Brazil's exit from its exchange-rate-based stabilization effort. It also meant that if developments ever did lead to a collapse of the Convertibility Plan, the consequences for the financial system and the Argentine economy were likely to be significantly more catastrophic than with a less rigid exchange rate and monetary policy regime.

However, the fundamental cause of Argentina's tragedy was not primarily the Convertibility Plan. Rather, it was the large and persistent excess of public spending over recurring revenues that led to an unsustainable accumulation of public debt and ultimately to sovereign default that fatally undermined the basis for Argentina's financial and economic stability—and would have done so under virtually any conceivable monetary policy and exchange rate regime.

Of course, the long recession that began in late 1998 made containment of Argentina's fiscal deficit and buildup of sovereign debt more difficult—both economically and politically. But, as was emphasized above, the fiscal problem started much earlier. If during each year of the past decade the primary balance of the entire Argentine government had been, on average, 2 percent of GDP better, the cumulative effect (including reduced interest expense) would have lowered Argentine sovereign debt in 2001 by about $60 billion. This would have removed any serious concerns about sovereign default and would have allowed significantly lower interest rates and a much better environment for economic recovery. Indeed, even moderately vigorous and realistic efforts of fiscal consolidation beginning with the recovery from the tequila crisis probably would have done the job. For example, an improvement in the primary balance of 1 percent of GDP in 1996, 2 percent of GDP in 1997, and 3 percent of GDP in 1998 should have been economically and politically feasible during these rapid-growth years; and holding on to an established fiscal improvement of 3 percent of GDP should have been achievable in the more difficult period of 1999–2001. This improvement in fiscal policy would have reduced Argentine debt in 2001 by about $40 billion (below the actual level), and it would have provided a convincing demonstration over six years of a capacity to run a more responsible fiscal policy. This should have been enough to remove serious doubts about fiscal sustainability. Thus, the margin between sustained success of Argentina's stabilization and reform efforts of the past decade and the tragic collapse at the end of 2001 was far from insurmountable.

Indeed, the tragedy in Argentina is epic not because, as in most Greek tragedies, it was inevitable, but because it was avoidable. After decades of generally poor economic performance and high inflation, punctuated by financial crises, the reforms of Carlos Menem and Domingo Cavallo delivered a sustained period of financial stability and economic progress. Inflation was banished. Despite the recession of 1995, for eight years, economic activity advanced at the highest average pace in a half-century. Trade was significantly liberalized. Inefficient public enterprises were privatized and compelled to become much more efficient. The banking system was put on a sound footing. A private pension system was established. The development of domestic capital markets was encouraged. And, as was proudly emphasized by President Menem in his address to the IMF-World Bank Annual Meetings in October 1998, the benefits of reform spread broadly: the number of Argentines living below the poverty line declined from 38 percent in 1989 to 18 percent; infant mortality fell by 27 percent; and 100 percent of children of school age attended primary school.

Thus reform accomplished a great deal—and promised to deliver more. But the fundamental failure to address adequately Argentina's persistent fiscal weakness—to a degree that was or should have been economically and politically feasible—ultimately undermined all of this progress and promise. Now, with sovereign default, with the collapse of the Convertibility Plan, with the failure of the financial system, and with the decline in the respect for law and rise in general distrust of government, Argentina faces its gravest economic crisis in at least a half-century: a true tragedy.

4

Looking Forward for Argentina

After passing through three interim presidents in barely ten days, the Argentine Congress elected Eduardo Duhalde, the losing Peronist presidential candidate in the 1999 election, to fill the remainder of President de la Rua's term. The new president immediately made two important decisions: he ratified the sovereign default announced by his short-lived predecessor (Rodriguez Saa), suspending debt-service payments to external creditors, together with a promise of future negotiations to reach a reasonable settlement; and he declared an official end to the Convertibility Plan and its one-to-one peg of the peso to the US dollar. Although the circumstances that led to these decisions were regrettable, by this stage there clearly was no viable alternative to either of them.

Unfortunately, the initial decisions of the Duhalde administration to try to maintain a dual exchange rate and to convert most bank loans, but not bank deposits, into pesos were based on political exigency rather than on sound economics. Within barely a month, economic reality forced the adoption of a unified floating exchange rate for foreign exchange transactions. The exchange rate for the conversion of dollar-denominated bank deposits, however, set a significantly higher value for such deposits than the market exchange rate applied for the conversion of dollar-denominated bank loans—implying huge capital losses and deep insolvency for Argentine banks. Also, a new bankruptcy law was passed that made it far more difficult for creditors to collect on defaulted claims, even if the debtor was potentially in a position to pay. And, a number of Argentine judges made use of an existing "economic subversion law" (dating back to Argentina's past governments and their efforts to suppress dissent) to pressure banks to release frozen deposits under threats of police action.

On a more positive note, the central government negotiated a deal with the provinces for a temporary reduction of transfers from the central government. But the deal involved the assumption by the central government of debts already issued by the provinces and failed to put an effective constraint on the provinces' authority to issue more debt, including debt that circulates as a money substitute. A budget for the central government that projected only a small fiscal deficit was proposed and passed by the Argentine Congress; but this budget was based on highly optimistic economic assumptions.

By mid-May 2002, some progress had been made by the Argentine authorities, including an agreement in principle between the president and provincial governors on a number of key issues. But the specific measures to implement these principles remained to be determined and enacted. Meanwhile, the economy minister, Remes Lenicov resigned when the Congress refused to adopt a key element of his plan to address the collapse of the banking system. All told, the efforts of the Argentine authorities continued to fall considerably short of a comprehensive, consistent, and credible program to achieve economic and financial stabilization and restore prosperity.

Recognizing the extremely challenging situation in Argentina, the international community, in particular the International Monetary Fund, should try to be as helpful as possible to the Argentine authorities in their efforts to stabilize the economy and put it on a path of sustainable growth. Most important, this can be done by making it clear that further meaningful financial assistance will be available to Argentina—on the condition that it develop and implement a consistent, responsible, and credible set of economic policies. This has been the central message of the international community, reinforced by the deliberations of the Fund's International Monetary and Finance Committee at its April 2002 ministerial meeting.

In accord with this approach, as the Argentine authorities make significant progress toward implementing their side of the bargain, it will be important that the international community, led by the Fund, be forthcoming concerning the support that they will be willing to supply and the specific conditions under which that support would be available. At the same time, it is essential to recognize that even with the best efforts of the Argentine authorities, backed by reasonable support from the international community, there is no assurance that stabilization and recovery will be achieved on the initial attempt. Indeed, the challenge is exceptionally difficult because the tragic collapse of the initially successful stabilization and reform efforts of the past decade have left the economy and the financial sector devastated. In addition, the government's credibility—even its legitimacy—has been seriously undermined by its failure to keep solemn commitments to its own citizens and to those who have invested in its economy and its securities. Undoubtedly, this critical problem has contributed to the delay in finding the political and social consensus essential for Argentina to move forward on the difficult measures necessary for stabilization and recovery. Unfortunately, delay and policy drift are only making the task more difficult.

The Prudent Level of International Support

In this situation, where the capacity of the Argentine authorities to deliver a consistent, responsible, and credible set of economic policies is likely to remain in substantial doubt, the international community must be prepared both to undertake some risks in supplying additional support and to act responsibly in controlling these risks. In this regard, key issues are how much support the Fund (and the international community) should be prepared to supply, over what period, and subject to what conditionality. The Argentine authorities undoubtedly want a very large amount of support to be provided very rapidly to help them to deal with the grave situation of the Argentine economy—subject to conditionality that recognizes immense economic and political difficulties of implementing a successful stabilization program. After all, if the Fund was prepared in 2000–01 to commit a large support package when the situation of Argentina was not as desperate as it is today, should it not be prepared to deliver the nondisbursed remainder of that package, plus a substantial augmentation?

Caving in to this type of argument would not be sound policy. A large support package was committed to Argentina in December 2000/January 2001 for a particular purpose: to give the Argentine authorities one last chance to implement policies that would avoid an economic and financial catastrophe. In keeping with this purpose, the level of support pledged to Argentina was well beyond the normal limits of Fund programs, and most of the support committed by the Fund was from the Supplemental Reserve Facility. This facility has a short maturity (repayment anticipated in one year and required in two years). As in other cases where the Fund has provided exceptionally large support, the idea was that a successful policy effort would enable the country to regain market access and rapidly repay the Fund. Unfortunately, in the case of Argentina, the policy effort failed.

Now, the situation is different. The Argentine economy is in far worse shape than it was in early 2001. But now Argentina does not face the threat of being cut off from private capital markets and the likelihood that this would induce sovereign default and a collapse of the Convertibility Plan. All of that has already happened. Hence, the large amounts of international support that were pledged to help avoid this outcome are no longer relevant. The issue is what level of assistance is appropriate now to

Table 4.1 Payments due to the IMF from Argentina, 2002–06

Payment category	2002	2003	2004	2005	2006
Principal due (millions of SDRs)	3,546	3,153	1,624	2,133	595
Interest and charges (millions of SDRs)	354	196	117	65	16
Total due (millions of SDRs)	3,900	3,349	1,741	2,198	611
Total due (millions of US dollars, at 1 SDR = $1.25)	4,875	4,186	2,176	2,747	764

SDR = special drawing right

Source: IMF Web site: http://www.imf.org.

support the Argentine government's new efforts at stabilization in the country's present situation.

Several important factors must be weighed in answering this question. The Fund already has substantial support outstanding to Argentina—nearly $14 billion. This amounts to 520 percent of Argentina's quota in the Fund, compared with a normal limit of 300 percent of quota for a member's total use of Fund resources. The already large level of Fund support for Argentina raises four concerns. First, as is indicated in table 4.1, Argentina is scheduled to make substantial repayments to the Fund during the next three years, and a default on these obligations would very seriously disrupt Argentina's relations with the international community. For the next year or two, however, it will clearly be very difficult for the Argentine government to secure the fiscal and foreign exchange resources to make scheduled repayments to the Fund (and other international financial institutions). Accordingly, it seems both reasonable and desirable for the Fund to extend sufficient credit to Argentina to finance the rollover of the repayments that are coming due to the Fund, provided that the Argentine authorities are making good-faith efforts to stabilize the situation.

Second, however, in extending additional credit (beyond rolling over scheduled repayments), the Fund has to take account of the fundamental responsibility to protect the temporary and revolving character of its support. When Fund support to a member is already very large, this is an important reason not to enlarge it further.

Third, in addition to protecting its resources, the Fund is also supposed to be governed by the general principle of "uniformity of treatment." Accordingly, a member that is already making much larger than normal use of Fund resources ought to be constrained in its use of additional Fund resources.

Fourth, even if the present efforts at stabilization in Argentina are highly successful, it is unlikely (especially in view of its sovereign default) that Argentina will rapidly reacquire voluntary access to private international capital markets. Thus, in the best of circumstances, Argentina will likely need support from the Fund for some time. And if present efforts at stabilization fall short of success, the future need for Fund resources will be even greater. In this situation, it would clearly be imprudent to commit all of the additional resources that the Fund might make available to Argentina to support the 2002 stabilization effort.

Beyond these concerns related to the scale of the Fund's existing support for Argentina, there are other important reasons why further extensions of official financial support should be kept within reasonable limits. In particular, approval of a new Fund-supported program while Argentina is in default on its sovereign obligations to private creditors would constitute "lending into arrears" to Argentina's private creditors. As a consequence of its default, Argentina will effectively receive a substantial flow of "exceptional financing," equal to the interest and principal payments that it is not making to its private foreign creditors. By lending into arrears, the Fund (on behalf of the international community) would recognize the need for, and signal official support of, this exceptional financing in the present circumstances of Argentina. But in so doing, the official international community must also insist that Argentina do its best to service these claims once the situation improves.

Indeed, official lending into the arrears of private creditors is necessarily a balancing act. Official support that assists in the stabilization of Argentina and in its more rapid return to economic prosperity will also increase the amounts that Argentina's private creditors are likely to receive on the obligations now in default. On the other hand, as the preferred creditor, the Fund (and other suppliers of official support) will surely and rightfully insist that their claims be fully serviced, and this potentially diminishes the resources available to meet the claims of Argentina's private creditors. Though the responsibility of the Fund is not to maximize returns to private creditors, it cannot serve the important interests of all its members in an efficiently functioning international financial system by ignoring the legitimate concerns of private creditors.

Moreover, in the case of Argentina, it is essential to recognize that the inability to control the appetite for public-sector borrowing was not only the primary cause of the present catastrophe, but it has also been a critical defect of Argentine public policy for decades. Thus, it would be perverse to believe that massive new public borrowing—this time from the Fund and the official international community—is the right way to resolve the present crisis. Official support is surely needed, but moderate levels of support ought to be sufficient. From the Fund, net new annual support (in addition to rolling over scheduled repayments) up to the normal limit of 100 percent of the Fund quota would supply about $2.7 billion, and net new money from the World Bank and the Inter-American Development Bank might raise the total of net new money to $4–5 billion.

On top of this, one should take some account of the "extraordinary financing" of $8–12 billion that Argentina will derive from deferral of payments of interest and principal on foreign debts. In addition, there will be revenue from money creation that will probably far exceed the limit of 3 billion pesos proposed in the government's budget. And it is reported that Argentina still has $12–14 billion in reserves, a modest part of which could be used to help finance the budget. Adding all of this up, the amount of financing is quite substantial for the government of a country whose GDP may be only about $150 billion (at the average exchange rate likely to prevail during 2002).

Bifurcated Conditionality

In considering the conditionality that should be applied in connection with new official financial support for Argentina from the Fund and other international financial institutions, it might be useful to distinguish between the conditionality appropriate for a rollover of existing support and the conditionality relevant for the extension of net new support. Under such a bifurcated system, conditionality appropriate for only a rollover of existing support would be somewhat more relaxed than usually applied; whereas conditionality applied for the extension of net new support would be at least as rigorous as that usually applied.

Under bifurcated conditionality, disbursements under an agreed-on program would proceed at the level of rollover plus significant new support only if the Argentine authorities were determined and generally successful in efforts to meet the program's objectives. If performance fell short of this rigorous standard, but the Argentine authorities were making good-faith efforts to implement the program, then disbursements could continue at the level of rollover of existing support. (Of course, if policy performance was clearly inadequate, disbursements would be interrupted until a new program, with appropriate prior actions, could be agreed on.)

Adoption of this form of bifurcated conditionality, however, would be an important departure from the principles, policies, and practices that govern conditionality (at least in the Fund) and might set precedents for cases beyond Argentina. Hence, it is important to weigh the potential benefits and defects. On the positive side, such bifurcated conditionality would recognize the very great difficulties confronting the Argentine authorities and would seek to avoid the serious problems that would arise if Argentina went into default on its obligations to the Fund or other international financial institutions. Also, it would be consistent with the Fund's sanctioning Argentina's deferral of debt service on its external private credits by lending into these arrears, if the Fund also recognized the implications of Argentina's very serious situation for its near-term ability to repay support previously extended by the Fund. It would recognize, however, that the Fund (and the other international financial institutions) have a clear obligation to protect their resources by requiring rigorous conditionality for further extensions of support, taking account of the substantial support that has already been extended to Argentina.

On the negative side, introduction of bifurcated conditionality in the Argentine case could imply a significant weakening of the tool of conditionality and could be seen as a violation of the principle of uniformity of treatment. Under the long-standing practices of the Fund, each new extension of Fund support is subject to conditionality during the period when that support is being disbursed, whether or not the member has payments due to the Fund arising from past support. Once disbursements cease, conditionality no longer applies, aside from the obligation of the member to make scheduled payments of interest and principal to the Fund. In seeking Fund support, all members stand on essentially the same footing, with no special preference given to members that already have outstanding support.

In contrast, under bifurcated conditionality, members with already outstanding support (especially large outstanding support) would appear to have an advantage in getting new support from the Fund, at least up to the level of the rollover of their already outstanding support. Moreover, under the principles implicit in bifurcated conditionality, the Fund and other international financial institutions would presumably have less leverage over members with already large outstanding support. Under the present system, such members have to earn the rollover of already outstanding support by accepting standard conditionality. Under bifurcated conditionality, members with large outstanding support would have more of a presumption in their favor in requesting rollovers of that support. For the Fund, this could mean a greater problem of some members making large and prolonged use of Fund resources—contrary to the principle that use of Fund resources should be temporary. For other international financial institutions that rely on borrowing in private credit markets for their financing, an apparent weakening of conditionality could mean higher financing costs, which would have to be passed on to all members using the resources of these institutions.

To put these concerns in proper perspective, however, it is essential to recognize that Argentina is a very special case in terms of the severity of its present crisis. The combination of sovereign default, collapse of the Convertibility Plan, virtual destruction of the domestic financial system, an exceptionally prolonged and deep decline in economic activity, and collapse of public confidence in government and the rule of law are—fortunately—not the concomitants of most the situations where members call upon the Fund for its support. Accordingly, the relevance of the Argentine case as a precedent for how conditionality should and will be handled in other cases may not be that great.

Requirements for Stabilization and Recovery

What should be the elements of the policy program that might be supported by moderate net new financing from the international community? Six elements can be delineated. First, the program should be based on realistically optimistic economic assumptions—on assumptions that presume success of the stabilization effort relative to Argentina's presently dire situation, but not on the absurdly optimistic assumptions in the government's recent budget. Even if stabilization efforts are successful and the downward economic spiral flattens out by midyear, Argentina's real GDP will likely fall 10 to 15 percent in 2002. The value of the peso has already (in mid-May) dropped below 30 US cents and is almost surely headed lower.

Indeed, even if a credible stabilization program were put in place at midyear and rigorously implemented, it is hard to see how the value of the peso at the end of 2002 could be kept above 20 or 25 US cents. Although the general increase in domestic prices (in pesos) would likely lag well behind the increase in the peso price of the dollar, nevertheless, domestic inflation on a December-to-December basis would appear to be headed over 200 percent. This may be an imprudently large number to admit explicitly in a Fund-supported program; but there in no point in denying that inflation in Argentina during 2002 is likely to be very high—even if hyperinflation in the thousands of percent is successfully avoided.

Second, given plausible economic assumptions, the government budget needs to be realistic and needs to include measures that will reasonably assure that the deficit will be within the bounds of what can be financed without resort to money (or money-substitute) creation at rates that will generate hyperinflation. The Argentine government will derive significant fiscal benefit from deferral of interest and principal payments on its external debt.[1]

Most debt service on the internal debt will need to be paid, however, if Argentine banks and pension funds that hold most of this debt are not to default on their obligations. Tax revenues are likely to be very low because of the economic collapse and very poor tax compliance—a problem that has been exacerbated by the general breakdown of respect for the government and for the rule of law. Also, there are likely to be substantial costs to the government from dealing with the mess it has created in the

---

1. Nonpayment of the interest on the external debt of perhaps $3–4 billion counts as a budgetary saving because interest expense normally appears as a budget expenditure. Nonpayment of principal is also a cash saving to the government and reduces the need for government financing (and balance of payments financing), but does not count as a budgetary saving in normal accounting. Also to the extent that interest and principal payments are deferred rather than written off, there are future budgetary and cash flow implications for temporary nonpayment of external debt-service obligations.

Argentine banking system. And there will be the politically difficult but absolutely essential task of reining in the deficits of the provinces and terminating their discretionary authority to borrow, virtually without constraint, by issuing debt that circulates as a money substitute.

All told, this suggests that containing pressures for deficit financing within tolerable limits will be very difficult. Official external financing and use of some of Argentina's foreign exchange reserves can probably finance a modest general government deficit. However, the creation of money and money substitutes will likely occur to a significantly greater extent than the planned issuance of 3 billion pesos; and use of such financing will need to be accepted, provided that it is contained within limits that will not drive inflation beyond tolerable limits. This probably means that the Fund will have to accept a bigger budget deficit and a higher inflation rate than it normally likes to see for countries receiving Fund support. For the Argentine authorities, it means slightly more slack on fiscal policy than would usually be acceptable in a Fund-supported program, but with the recognition that the results of the stabilization effort are likely to be less satisfactory than the Argentine authorities would like to admit. The point is to have a program that has at least some chance of being successfully implemented—a program that is not virtually assured of collapsing with further damage to the Argentine government's already tattered credibility—a program on which the Argentine authorities will be required to deliver or face interruptions in the flow of international support.

Third, it is essential to establish a reasonable framework for monetary policy. The Argentine authorities have indicated that monetary policy (of the operationally independent Central Bank of Argentina) will be governed by an inflation target. This sounds like a reasonable policy for 2004 and beyond, after stabilization efforts have succeeded in restoring growth, in reducing inflation to moderate rates, and in resurrecting the Argentine financial system. (Mexico, for example, was able to move successfully to inflation targeting a couple of years after the tequila crisis. Brazil moved very rapidly to inflation targeting after the crisis of early 1999; but the crisis in Brazil was not nearly as catastrophic as the present crisis in Argentina.)

However, in 2002 and probably also in 2003, the Central Bank of Argentina will have great difficulty in controlling the supply of money and central bank credit, and the demand for domestic money is likely to be highly unstable. The central bank will simply not have the means to keep inflation within relatively narrow bounds of a preannounced target; and announcing that the objective of monetary policy is to keep inflation in the range of, say, 150 to 250 percent is not a meaningful prescription for an inflation target.

Rather, the objective of monetary policy should be to contain the initial inflationary surge from the collapsing value of the peso and then bring the inflation rate down to more moderate levels during the course of the next two years. This will require that the central bank strictly limit the growth of its own credit to within boundaries agreed on for the Fund-supported program and, consistent with these quantitative limits, will generally imply interest rates on central bank credit be kept at levels that are generally positive in real terms. In addition, monetary policy will clearly need the support of fiscal policy to keep public debt issuance within tolerable limits and to lend credibility to the notion that monetary policy will not be completely dominated by the needs of public finance.

Fourth, exchange rate policy needs to be adapted to deal with the present crisis. The initial attempt of the Duhalde government to institute (for an interim period of several months) a dual exchange rate (with the rate for most trade transactions pegged at 1.4 pesos to the US dollar) was a serious mistake. Not only was this system doomed to collapse, as it did in a few weeks, but its inevitable collapse further undermined the government's limited credibility.

A unified floating exchange rate for the peso is the only reasonable option in present circumstances. Official intervention can be appropriate to counteract turbulence in the foreign exchange market; but intervention should not be consistently one-sided, should not attempt to defend any specific exchange rate, and should not be permitted to result in substantial losses of Argentina's official reserves. It must be recognized that given everything else that is happening in Argentina, the peso inevitably will depreciate very substantially (from its old parity) in real terms—and even more so in nominal terms.

As in other countries where exchange rate pegs have collapsed, depreciation will be "excessive" in the period following the collapse, and the real exchange rate will likely recover to more reasonable levels as the crisis abates. The principal policy tool to resist "overly excessive" depreciation is not large-scale official intervention, but rather the maintenance of sufficiently tight conditions on the supply of domestic credit. In addition, temporary controls on capital outflows may be useful, although such controls are distortive, tend to lose effectiveness over time, and afford opportunities for corruption.

Fifth, something needs to be done to clean up the horrendous mess in the Argentine banking system—for without a functioning banking system it will be very difficult to restore reasonable prosperity to the Argentine economy. In approaching this problem, it is essential to recognize that the responsibility for the mess lies entirely with the Argentine government—both past and present. Four actions of the Argentine government have made the Argentine banking system effectively insolvent and incapable of meeting the claims of depositors: (1) The government defaulted on its commitments to honor its own dollar-denominated debt, including substantial amounts of such debt held by Argentine banks. (2) The government reneged on its commitment to maintain the Convertibility Plan, leading to a massive depreciation of the peso against the dollar. (3) The government mandated that dollar-denominated loans of Argentine banks were payable in pesos. (4) The government mandated that dollar-denominated deposits at Argentine banks be converted into pesos at an exchange rate for the peso much above that used to convert dollar-denominated bank loans.

It has already been argued that by no later than mid-2001, the first two of these actions had become unavoidable. The third action was a wise recognition of the fact that after the collapse of the Convertibility Plan most Argentine debtors would not be able to service their dollar-denominated loans from Argentine banks. The first three actions together effectively forced a massive write-down in the dollar value of the assets held by Argentine banks—a write-down that was unavoidable. If, instead of the fourth action, the dollar value of the liabilities (and capital) of Argentine banks had been converted into pesos (at the same one-to-one exchange rate as dollar-denominated bank loans), the banking system would have remained solvent.[2]

The Argentine government, however, lacked the political courage to tell the Argentine people the truth: that the US dollar value of their deposits in Argentine banks was being sharply reduced as a result of government actions. Instead, through the fourth action, the Argentine government sought to purvey the fiction that most of the dollar value of deposits could be preserved as the peso depreciated and to shift the blame for the losses of depositors from the government to Argentine banks.

Now, the Argentine public has, with good reason, lost confidence in the banking system and has little reason for confidence in the government or any of its promises. Moreover, the owners of Argentine banks who have effectively been robbed of all of their invested capital also have little reason to believe any promises of the Argentine government. This means that there is no incentive for these bank owners, or any who might succeed them, to put in new capital to refloat the banking system—that would simply be an invitation to be robbed again by the Argentine government.

One possibility would be for the international community to supply the resources (perhaps $10 billion or $15 billion) to recapitalize the Argentine banking system and lend its credibility to support renewed public confidence in that system. That, however, would be an unconscionable mistake. Beyond the general reasons why further international support for

---

2. This was the essence of the proposal made by Ricardo Hausmann (Personal View, *Financial Times*, October 30, 2001). It was widely recognized well before the event that the collapse of the Convertibility Plan would inevitably cause great problems for the Argentine banking system. The only sensible way to deal with these problems was to convert both dollar-denominated bank assets and dollar-denominated bank liabilities into pesos at the same one-to-one rate, and then allow the dollar value of both bank assets and liabilities to depreciate along with the dollar value of the peso.

Argentina should be kept within reasonable limits, it is essential that the international community not lend its financial or moral support to bail the Argentine government out of a predicament that is so clearly the result of its own cynical misbehavior.

Rather, the burden must be on the Argentine government to find the bulk of the resources, within a tightly constrained budget, that are needed to recapitalize the banking system. This could probably be done most efficiently by supplying public funds to limit the losses of bank owners to no more than half or two-thirds of their invested capital, and by attempting to persuade them to supply some additional capital to help refloat the banking system. To help restore public confidence in the banking system, the government should also admit forthrightly the fundamental causes of the system's recent failure and seek to provide some assurance that similar mistakes will be avoided in the future. When the Argentine government has a responsible plan to address the problems in the banking system, the international community should consider providing some meaningful assistance to support that endeavor.

Sixth, the Argentine authorities need to signal their clear intention to pursue good-faith efforts to deal responsibly with their external sovereign debt and with a host of obligations to foreigners (such as contractual commitments to foreign investors in Argentine utilities) in which they are now in default. Two general principles should be recognized as governing how these problems will ultimately be resolved: (1) Argentina's foreign private creditors and other private holders of contractual claims on Argentina will need to recognize that in the ultimate resolution of their claims, they will not be made whole, but rather will need to share in the enormous economic losses being sustained by the Argentine economy in the present crisis. Private foreign investors in Argentina undertook risks when they made their investments, and generally they were promised rates of return that reflected these risks. As with all investors who undertake risks anywhere, when things turn out particularly badly, investors (including bond holders and others secured by contractual obligations) take losses. (2) The Argentine authorities must ensure that foreign investors in Argentina are treated "fairly" in the sense that they are not forced to accept disproportionately large losses. What constitutes fair treatment in individual cases will need to be a subject of negotiation and likely a matter of dispute. But treatment that falls substantially short of Argentina's reasonable best efforts to meet its external obligations across a broad front should not be that difficult to discern. The international community has the right and the obligation to insist, as one of the conditions for its support, that the Argentine authorities assiduously apply these principles in dealing with their external obligations.

Of course, the resolution of most of the private claims on Argentina will not occur quickly. Because of the dire state of the economy and of the government's budget, the resources to meet external claims are now very limited. And seeking to negotiate now how most external claims will be resolved on the basis of promises of what will be done when the economic and budgetary situations improve is unlikely to be very productive. The uncertainties for both sides in such bargains are simply too great to make any deal credible and mutually acceptable.

When the economic situation does stabilize and the Argentine economy moves forward into recovery, then the time for serious negotiations with external claimants will begin. At that stage, Argentina will not yet have regained voluntary access to private credit markets and will likely still be dependent on the Fund and the rest of the official international community for support (or at least for rollovers of past support). Thus, the international community will still have considerable leverage over the Argentine authorities; and, if necessary, it should be prepared to use this leverage to help assure than external claimants on Argentina are treated fairly.

This approach is consistent with—indeed, it is required by—the Fund's fundamental responsibility to provide assistance to its members while simultaneously supporting the principles of a stable and efficient international financial system and safeguarding the temporary revolving character of its own resources. The exceptionally difficult circumstances confronting the Argentine authorities argue for Fund support to be as generous as possible, under appropriate conditionality.

Because outstanding Fund support for Argentina is already substantial, however, it is particularly important to assure that further extensions of support do not expose the Fund to undue risks. A strong policy program that is vigorously implemented by the Argentine authorities is the most important protection against these risks—because it is the indispensable requirement to restore stability and renew prosperity in Argentina. But the situation is so difficult that it is essential to recognize that, despite the best efforts of the Argentine authorities, success may not be achieved on the first attempt. As the unfortunate experience with the large disbursement of August–September 2001 clearly demonstrates, it would be a serious mistake to venture large amounts of whatever additional support the Fund might reasonably supply to Argentina on one-shot efforts that may fall well short of what is needed for sustainable success.

5

Lessons for the Fund

If the International Monetary Fund is to recover and improve as a useful instrument of the international community, it must learn from the experience of its involvement with Argentina during the past decade. Such learning must begin with the recognition that though the tragic failure of Argentina's initially successful efforts at economic stabilization was primarily the consequence of what Argentina did and did not do, it also reflects important mistakes by the Fund. If these mistakes were isolated errors, their significance for the Fund's general operations would be limited. However, there has been a great deal of criticism of the Fund across a wide range of its operations during the past decade. Though much of this criticism, in my opinion, has been misinformed, misguided, and in some cases mean-spirited, the mistakes that the Fund made in Argentina are not isolated errors. Rather, they reflect wider deficiencies that merit careful diagnosis and serious efforts to find remedies.

Tough Cop or Sympathetic Social Worker?

To understand why the Fund made important mistakes in Argentina and limit the future risk of similar mistakes, it is essential to recognize the fundamental tension between two key roles that the Fund is expected to play in the international economic system. The Fund is expected to serve the interests of its members, individually and collectively, by acting both as a sympathetic social worker and as a tough cop. As a sympathetic social worker, the Fund provides friendly advice to its members about their economic policies and provides financial assistance in times of actual or potential difficulties. The advice must, of course, take note of policy deficiencies, but it should be cognizant both of the political difficulties of implementing necessary but unpopular measures and of the political and financial market sensitivity of any public criticism. To be most effective in reassuring financial markets at times of actual or potential crisis, the Fund's financial support should be available in large amounts, with sympathetic understanding of situations when policy measures fall somewhat short of their objectives, and without much emphasis on the possibility of interruptions in assistance if Fund-supported programs go seriously off track.

On the other hand, as the tough cop of the international financial system, the Fund is expected to point out explicitly (and in the new age of transparency, also publicly) key deficiencies in the economic policies of its members. Its financial assistance to members is supposed to be limited to the "catalytic role" of filling in modest financing gaps that might remain after account is taken of the effect of a member's adjustment program in restoring market confidence. For this purpose, Fund financial support should be tightly conditioned on a rigorous program of adjustment measures, with vigorous actions required to correct any deficiencies in meeting program objectives.

Much of the popular discontent with the Fund, especially in countries that have operated under Fund-supported programs, is that the Fund is overzealous in its role as a tough cop, rather than overindulgent in its role as a sympathetic social worker. In fact, the reverse is far more often the case—as a moment's reflection on the nature of the Fund should reveal.

The Fund exists to serve its members. In their individual interactions with the Fund, virtually all members prefer to deal with the sympathetic social worker rather than the tough cop. Even industrial countries that no longer expect to make much use of financial support from the Fund do not usually appreciate criticism, especially public criticism, of their policies. Developing countries that do or might make use of Fund resources are generally even less enthusiastic about the Fund as a tough cop—as applied to them individually. Applied to others, of course, members see important virtues in an effective policeman. Even users of Fund resources must recognize that if the conditionality associated with Fund support is seen as a travesty, its value in helping to restore confidence will be seriously undermined. Nevertheless, the preference of countries about how they would like to be treated individually as members of the Fund undoubtedly holds sway.

It is not surprising that the preferences of members affect how the Fund operates. Inevitably, the incentives for the Fund staff and management and most individual members of the Executive Board (although not usually the Executive Board as a collective) are to lean sympathetically toward the preferences of members. This tendency is not absolute. The Fund does criticize members' policies, often quite forcefully and sometimes in public. Fund financial support is usually provided in moderate amounts and is subject to relevant conditionality. It is not unusual for disbursements under established Fund programs to be interrupted, sometimes for brief periods and sometimes for extended periods, when programs go off track.

But the tendency in the Fund is to give the benefit of the doubt, sometimes the overwhelming benefit of the doubt, to the member. And because this tendency is the consequence of the preferences of the membership and the incentives to serve those preferences, it persists despite the generally high level of professional competence and dedication of the Fund's staff and management and its executive directors.

This tendency was clearly apparent in the case of Argentina. Initial doubts about the desirability and viability of the Convertibility Plan were suppressed after it passed the crucial test of the tequila crisis, notwithstanding the longer-term difficulties and risks that this arrangement might pose for the Argentine economy. This was plausibly justified under the important principle that it is the right of a member to determine its own exchange rate and monetary policy regime. This excuse, however, does not apply to what I have argued to be the Fund's inadequate attention to the failures of Argentine fiscal policy. Indeed, the rigid constraints of the Convertibility Plan clearly made a potentially unsustainable fiscal policy an even greater danger for Argentina. Accordingly, this should have intensified the Fund's critical focus on the failures of Argentina's fiscal policy.

Improving the Fund's Accountability and Performance

How might the Fund's performance in such situations be improved? In my view, something is clearly needed to counterbalance the tendency of the Fund to act too much as a sympathetic social worker—without going too far in the other direction. Specifically, there need to be better mechanisms of decision making and of accountability in the Fund: mechanisms that provide more effective checks and balances to assure that decisions are made on the basis of the best possible analysis, not analysis that is biased by a desire to see things from the member's point of view; and mechanisms that provide for careful appraisal of the Fund's performance in critical cases and, when mistakes have been made, appropriately assess (in some detail) the responsibility for those mistakes.

One possibility would be to alter the Fund's internal practices and bureaucratic organization to give less of a bias toward positive assessments of members' economic performance and policies. The Fund's area departments are responsible for maintaining its key relations with its members and for preparing the documents for its surveillance and programs. This has been an efficient arrangement which has contributed importantly to the Fund's effectiveness as an international organization.

However, by the nature of their responsibilities and because of their need and desire to maintain close cooperative relations with the authorities of member countries, the bias toward the member tends to be particularly strong in the Fund's area departments. Other departments that review and comment on the work of the area departments should counterbalance their natural bias. But because the area departments control the word processor in drafting key documents, the counterbalancing effect tends to be muted. The Fund's management is supposed to settle differences among the staff; and it approves all key documents. However, in my experience, management normally sides with the area departments in their efforts to be as cooperative with members as possible.

The Executive Board is rarely informed of differences in views among the staff; it only sees the finally approved documents and hears (on country matters) the staff of the area departments. Thus, although the Executive Board has different interests and incentives as a collective entity than those of individual executive directors in trying to serve the specific interests of the individual members that they represent, its role as a counterbalance to the bias to see things from the individual member's short-term perspective is also compromised.

Accordingly, a change in these procedures that allowed for a more fully informed Executive Board—one better able to perceive the biases in the work of the staff and management—might imply a somewhat greater incentive for management to insist on a balanced view and to value constructive dissent in the work of the staff. This, in turn, would tend to diminish the bias of the Fund toward seeing things in the best possible light from the perspective of the member.

Another important means of improving accountability is to make good use of the Fund's independent evaluation office, which has just started to operate. Because it functions under the authority of the Fund's Executive Board, independent of staff and management, this office should be relatively free of the natural human tendency of those most directly responsible for the Fund's operations to see their own work as largely error free and not subject to any undesirable biases. However, as an agency within the broader institutional framework of the Fund and ultimately responsible to the Fund's membership, the effective independence and integrity of the evaluation office remain to be demonstrated.

Clearly, analysis and assessment of the Fund's performance in Argentina will be a key challenge for the new evaluation office. It is to be hoped that it will choose to undertake this challenge within the next year or so and make its report promptly and publicly available. Quite possibly, such an evaluation will not agree entirely with what is said in this policy analysis. However, it seems highly implausible that an honest and rigorous appraisal could conclude that the Fund made no serious mistakes in its involvement with Argentina during the past decade. Because the deterioration of Argentina's public finances ultimately led to the largest sovereign default in history, and because this default plays an important role in Argentina's other miseries, surely a careful appraisal of the Fund's efforts to influence Argentina's fiscal policy appears essential. Other issues, including the Fund's analysis and advice concerning Argentina's Convertibility Plan, also deserve to be on the agenda.

Indeed, a comprehensive assessment of Fund's work on all significant issues in the Argentine case is important to avoid drawing the wrong conclusions. For example, it is my view that the Argentine government's basic decision to combine efforts at macroeconomic stabilization with market-oriented reforms that reversed decades of interventionist policies and protectionism was the right policy approach, and that the Fund was right to support this approach.

In accord with this view, the spectacular success of the Argentine economy throughout most of the past decade is attributable to this basic policy choice; and the spectacular collapse in 2001 is due to the failure to implement this strategy sufficiently vigorously, especially in the area of achieving and maintaining adequate fiscal discipline. Others, however, may be inclined to the view that the policies of the so-called Washington consensus are fundamentally wrong and were doomed from the start to produce a disaster in Argentina. An evaluation of the Fund's role in Argentina should reflect on this broad question.

Issues concerning Argentina's fiscal, monetary, and exchange rate policies lie at the heart of the Fund's typical concerns with its member's macroeconomic policies, and the appraisal of the Fund's work on these issues concerns primarily the work of the relevant staff and effectiveness of the supervision provided by management. As was emphasized in chapter 1, the Argentine case is particularly noteworthy, relative to most other cases where the Fund has provided exceptionally large financial support, in the extent to which the key policy concerns were those that lie at the heart of the Fund's traditional responsibilities and expertise. Accordingly, a carefully critical evaluation of the performance of the Fund's staff and management in this case is potentially of considerable significance for a more general assessment of how the Fund does its assigned job and what may be needed to improve its performance in its central areas of responsibility.

Another key issue in the Argentine case is the appropriateness of the decision to provide exceptionally large Fund support to Argentina that was made in December 2000 (and approved by the Executive Board in January 2001) and of the decision to significantly augment that support made in August 2001 (and approved by the Executive Board in September 2001). Here the main responsibility rests with Fund management and with key officials in leading Fund members who were actively involved in making or approving these decisions. No report on the Fund's involvement in Argentina would be complete or credible without forthright discussion of these issues.

The Role of Large Support Packages

Beyond an appraisal of whether large-scale assistance to Argentina was appropriate in the particular circumstances of that case, there are also some important implications for the general policy issues associated with large-scale financial assistance packages. In my view, one useful suggestion is to require that the Fund (staff and management) prepare a special, formal justification for any proposal to extend support to a member beyond the normal limits of access to Fund resources (100 percent of Fund quota in any single year, and a cumulative maximum of 300 percent of quota).

In connection with this justification, it would also be useful to indicate (to the Executive Board, but not publicly) expectations concerning substantial policy adjustments that the member might be required to undertake if a program backed by exceptionally large Fund support began to go seriously off track. For example, in connection with the large support package of December 2000/January 2001, the Argentine authorities should have been told explicitly (but privately) that if the program backed by this support package went seriously off track (as it clearly did by the summer of 2001), then a compulsory restructuring of Argentina's sovereign debt and possibly a substantial alteration in the Convertibility Plan would need to be implemented.

Under the Fund's established policies, support beyond the normal limits of access is supposed to occur only in "exceptional circumstances." What constitutes exceptional circumstances has never been defined; and, in my view, it would be a mistake to try to define this term in a general way and then apply it to individual cases. In individual cases, however, it should be possible to say explicitly what makes them exceptional enough to justify Fund support beyond the normal limits. It would be appropriate within the Fund's usual procedures to require that the Fund staff and management make this justification explicit to the Fund's Executive Board.

I would also suggest that all cases of exceptional access should be reviewed, ex post, by the independent evaluation office—both concerning their general features and consequences and with respect to the justification for exceptional access. Suggestions that super-majority votes of the Executive Board should be required to approve programs with exceptional access, however, do not appear to be either useful or appropriate. In fact, decisions by the Executive Board on Fund programs are taken by consensus; and there are few instances where any executive director votes no on a program recommended by management (although executive directors do sometimes exercise considerable influence on Fund programs before they are submitted for formal approval).

Since the large support package arranged for Mexico in 1995, these operations have been the subject of a great deal of comment and criticism. The key concern has been that a policy of providing such packages to countries facing external financing crises tends to generate moral hazard that may make such crises more likely. Specifically, expectations of the large-scale official support may encourage either countries or their creditors to undertake imprudent risks because they expect that, in the event of crisis, the international community will step in and shield them from an important part of the losses they would otherwise have to absorb.

To deal with this perceived problem, a number of proposals have been advanced to eliminate or curtail large-scale support packages or to structure them in ways that would better control problems of moral hazard. These proposals cover a wide range—including abolition of the Fund; replacement of traditional Fund lending to countries in difficulty with prequalified credit extended only to countries with outstanding economic policies; and limitation of Fund support to the normal level of 100 percent of Fund quota, with the requirement that amounts above this limit be conditioned on a restructuring of a country's external debt.

In particular, the Report of the International Financial Institutions Advisory Commission, generally know as the Meltzer Commission report was generally quite critical of the Fund's operations in recent financial crises. The commission's majority recommended scrapping the Fund's traditional approach of providing support. Specifically, in contrast with current practice, the Fund would not provide support to countries in crisis or facing an immediate threat of crisis, subject to conditionality on policies to address that actual or potential crisis. Instead, to encourage countries to have good policies that would effectively avoid potential crises, the Fund should be prepared to pre-commit large packages of support to those countries judged to have outstanding economic policies. (Almost by definition, such countries would not face crises at the time that Fund support was initially committed, although they might later face the threat of contagion from countries that did not have outstanding policies.) Policies to create and maintain a sound domestic banking and financial system, including liberal rules for participation of foreign banks, were given special importance. In contrast, the need for a sound fiscal policy was only added as an afterthought to the commission's majority view.

On the criterion of having a sound banking system, with widespread participation of foreign banks, Argentina was clearly outstanding (ignoring what might happen in the event of sovereign default or collapse of the Convertibility Plan), and it was particularly praised in this regard by one of the members of the Meltzer Commission's majority. Presumably, on these grounds, under the commission's proposals, Argentina would have qualified for a very large package of pre-committed support.

If most of what has been argued in this book is mainly correct, however, it clearly would have been a serious mistake to pre-commit a huge package of support for Argentina primarily on the basis of its sound banking system—and effectively ignore the risks of sovereign default and collapse of the Convertibility Plan implicit in an inadequately disciplined fiscal policy. Moreover, if the Meltzer Commission proposals were now applied to Argentina, with its wrecked banking system and collapsing economy, the implication would presumably be that no substantial Fund support should be committed to Argentina, regardless of the policies of the Argentine government, until a sound banking system is restored—which can probably only occur after the present deep crisis is largely resolved.

More generally, in my view, concerns about moral hazard have been vastly exaggerated, and most of the proposals to deal with this purported problem (including those of the Meltzer Commission) are unnecessary, unworkable, or fundamentally misguided. The Argentine case is particularly relevant in this regard. When a country experiences a financial crisis, it typically suffers very substantial economic damage. International financial support should help to ameliorate that damage; but it is absurd to think that expectations of such support are an important inducement for countries to run the risk of such crises.

Indeed, in the case of Argentina, the key policy decisions that created the risk of a catastrophic crisis were the decisions to adopt and maintain the Convertibility Plan and the cumulative decisions that led to an unsustainable fiscal policy even when the Argentine economy was performing well. These decisions were made well before there was any question of large-scale financial support from the Fund, and it is implausible to suggest that they were meaningfully influenced by expectations of such support.

Most foreign investors also suffer substantial economic damage when a country experiences an external financing crisis. This includes most owners of direct investments and portfolio equity investments, as well as holders of longer-term bonds that sell out when market values decline sharply during a crisis. However, some foreign investors are usually able to escape large losses when there is a crisis, and they are aided in doing so by the availability of official financial support. Specifically, holders of short-term credits (especially interbank credits) are often able to get out without large losses, and owners of longer-term credits (especially of sovereign credits) may come out whole if they hold their positions and default is ultimately avoided.

So what? In private capital markets in industrial economies such as the United States, when a business firm gets into financial difficulty, many short-term creditors are often able to get out without significant loss. Indeed, businesses frequently arrange secondary lines of credit to help finance an exit of their normal suppliers of short-term credit if the suppliers of such credit become nervous. Also, when businesses need to restructure their finances without the firm actually going insolvent, bondholders often do quite well, while the claims of equity owners are seriously diluted or even wiped out. Thus, efficient functioning of advanced capital markets and containment of moral hazard do not require that, when a borrower experiences difficulties, all of the claimants on a business' capital suffer losses or that such losses be similar across different types of claimants. Of course, when a firm is deeply insolvent, all claimants on its capital (except those that have already gotten out or hold claims secured by specific assets) may expect to suffer substantial losses—although generally not in the same proportion.

Presumably, international capital markets should function in a similar manner. Argentina is a particularly noteworthy case in this regard. Substantial official support was committed to Argentina in December 2000–January 2001 in an effort to give the Argentine authorities one last chance to demonstrate fiscal prudence, restore market confidence, and avoid catastrophe. Even with the unwise augmentation of official support in August/September 2001, however, the level of official support clearly remained well below that which would provide an effective bailout for the bulk of Argentina's private creditors.

Indeed, the Argentine sovereign did ultimately default on a large volume of private credit. And, as one would want and expect in an efficiently functioning capital market, virtually all investors in Argentina (except those who got out early) will have to absorb very large losses. This includes holders of short-term credits and holders of sovereign bonds that, in many financial crises, escape with comparatively modest losses.

Were there not, at least occasionally, a case like Argentina, private investors might conclude that there was virtually no risk from investing in sovereign bonds of emerging-market countries. But a case like Argentina, and Russia before it, teaches a powerful lesson that even politically important emerging-market countries do sometimes default on their sovereign bonds. Indeed, while global financial markets reacted with shock and surprise to Russia's default in August 1998 because it was widely believed that Russia was "too nuclear" to be allowed to fail, the general financial market reaction to Argentina's default has been quite muted. Apparently, markets do understand that there are significant risks in investing in emerging markets, including in sovereign credits; and they recognize that these risks will sometimes materialize in substantial losses.

To be clear, it would not have been appropriate to limit international support for Argentina to provoke a sovereign default because that was useful or necessary to send a message to private capital markets. If the policy efforts of the Argentine authorities supported by the financial package of December 2000/January 2001 had succeeded in containing the fiscal deficit, restoring financial market confidence, and avoiding a sovereign default and a collapse of the Convertibility Plan, that clearly would have been a much better outcome. But, given that a catastrophic crisis proved unavoidable, it is right to take note of the lessons that such a crisis teaches about market discipline.

Moreover, Argentina is not the first, and is unlikely to be the last, emerging-market borrower to be forced into sovereign default and an associated deep economic and financial crisis. Although not usually as great as in the case of Argentina, the costs of such crises are typically huge. It is difficult to believe that we need to encourage more such crises than we are otherwise likely to see to keep within acceptable bounds the problems of moral hazard likely to arise from international support provided by the Fund and other international financial institutions.

Finally, it should be emphasized that if exceptional support from the Fund and the international community is to play its appropriate role in limiting the risk of and damage from potential and actual financial crises, it must be used with competent discretion. Sometimes, as in the large-scale assistance provided to Mexico by the Fund and the US Treasury during the tequila crisis, such assistance will succeed in supporting the determined efforts of the national policy authorities to avoid an unnecessarily disastrous crisis, as would have followed in the wake of a Mexican sovereign default.

In other cases, such as South Korea during the Asian crisis, large-scale official assistance may be effectively and efficiently combined with constructive actions to enlist private-sector creditors to support credible policy efforts to contain and reverse a financial crisis. In yet other cases, such as (arguably) Argentina in late 2000, it may be worth the risk to commit large-scale official assistance to support efforts to avoid a disastrous outcome, even if it later turns out that those efforts fall short. But there will also be cases, such as Russia in August 1998 and Argentina by the summer of 2001, where there is no realistic hope of sufficiently determined policy actions that will rescue a desperate situation; in such cases, provision of large-scale official assistance is a mistake. The task of the Fund, on behalf of the international community, is to exercise competent discretion in distinguishing between these situations and acting appropriately.

Appendix A
The Fund Staff Analysis of Argentina's Sovereign Debt Dynamics

The sustainability of Argentina's debt dynamics clearly became an important issue in 2000–01, and the International Monetary Fund staff provided an analysis of this issue in its reports on the Fund's program with Argentina. The staff report of August 2001 supporting the Fund's decision to proceed with a large augmentation of Fund assistance for Argentina has not, unfortunately, been publicly released; and its analysis of Argentina's debt dynamics at this critical juncture is therefore not publicly available. However, the staff report on the May 2001 review of the Fund program with Argentina (which recommended waivers of missed first-quarter performance criteria and modification of performance criteria for the second quarter, in order to proceed with the program) was publicly released as IMF Country Report 01/90 in June 2001 and is available at the IMF Web site, http://www.imf.org/external/pubs/ft/scr/2001/cr0190. pdf. The analysis in this report is revealing about how the Fund's staff analyzed this issue and what it was prepared to say about it in its report to the Executive Board.

The relevant paragraph in that report states:

> Given the authorities commitment to meet the deficit requirements of the fiscal responsibility law of 2001 and beyond, the debt *dynamics analysis remains broadly unaffected* [compared with the previous staff report], assuming that economic activity recovers as envisaged. Valuation changes in the fourth quarter raised the outstanding stock of debt at end-2000 by about 1 percentage point of GDP, to almost 51 percent of GDP. Based on conservative growth and interest rate assump-

tions, the debt/GPD ratio will continue to rise until 2002, partly reflecting continued recognition of past liabilities—when it peaks at about 54.5 percent of GDP. It will start to decline steadily thereafter, but will still be above 50 percent by 2005 (Table 7). As shown in the report for the second review, the debt dynamics are particularly sensitive to the rate of growth of GDP, and less to variations in the interest rate, given the relatively high average maturity of the public debt.

The footnote to the text describing the "conservative growth and interest rate assumptions" states, "It is assumed that growth will gradually accelerate to reach 4¼ percent by 2003. The interest rate on new borrowing reflects the large participation of official lenders in 2001–02, and a rate on market borrowing that starts in the 13–14 percent range in 2001 and declines gradually to about 10 percent by 2005."

Table 7 from this staff report is quite interesting and is reproduced here as table A.1. What should be made of this analysis? The general principle in such matters is that if you are prepared to swallow the assumptions, then you should also eat the conclusions. Or, as we used to say when I was growing up, "If, if, if . . . If my grandmother had wheels, she would be a bus."

As is revealed in the table, the Fund's staff *assumes* that real GDP growth for Argentina will be 2.0 percent in 2001, 3.7 percent in 2003, and 4.3 percent thereafter. But by mid-May 2001, it was abundantly clear that the recession was continuing to deepen in Argentina, and –2 percent growth would have been a more reasonable forecast than +2 percent. There was no evidence of imminent economic recovery, and both the high level of interest rates and the assumed degree of further fiscal tightening suggested continued economic contraction through 2002.

On interest rates, the Fund staff analysis *assumes* that the interest rate on new federal debt would run between 10 and 11.5 percent through 2004. At the time of the staff report, market interest rates on Argentine sovereign debt with maturities running out for 20 years were in the range of 14 to 16 percent.

On the Argentine government's fiscal policy, the Fund staff analysis *assumes* that the "fiscal responsibility law," which placed an absolute cap on the stock of government debt, would be effectively implemented and enforced, despite the absence of concrete measures to achieve this result or any realistic prospect that it would be achieved. As is discussed in the main text, under more plausible assumptions about real growth, about interest rates facing the Argentine sovereign (assuming that it could access private credit markets at all), and about achievable degree of fiscal discipline, by mid-May 2001, Argentina's ratio of sovereign debt to GDP appeared to be headed off toward the wild blue yonder.

Of course, there is room for reasonable disagreement about what are the right assumptions concerning real growth, interest rates, and achievable fiscal outcomes. And a sensible analysis of sovereign debt dynamics should probably contemplate a range of plausible results. But there is a

Table A.1 Argentina: Consolidated public sector debt dynamics (in millions of US dollars)

	1997	1998	1999	2000	2001 (projected)	2002 (projected)	2003 (projected)	2004 (projected)	2005 (projected)
Debt, beginning of period	108,318	111,547	123,508	134,270	144,805	157,265	165,563	171,502	174,791
Primary balance	788 (0.3)	1,543 (0.5)	−2,133 (−0.8)	1,308 (0.5)	4,642 (1.6)	8,081 (2.7)	11,467 (3.6)	14,973 (4.5)	17,492 (5.0)
Interest payments	6,843 (2.3)	7,858 (2.6)	9,655 (3.4)	11,512 (4.0)	13,902 (4.7)	14,979 (4.9)	16,006 (5.0)	17,062 (5.1)	17,492 (5.0)
Overall balance	−6,055 (−2.1)	−6,315 (−2.1)	−11,788 (−4.2)	−10,205 (−3.6)	−9,260 (−3.1)	−6,898 (−2.3)	−4,539 (−1.4)	−2,089 (−0.6)	0 (0.0)
Privatization receipts[1]	1,264	558	889	166	400	200	200	100	100
Debt consolidation (recognition)	942	1,123	1,546	1,513	2,100	1,400	1,400	1,100	1,000
Other debt creating flows[2]	−2,504	5,081	−1,683	−1,017	1,500	200	200	200	200
Debt, end of period	111,547 (38.1)	123,508 (41.3)	134,270 (47.4)	144,805 (50.8)	157,265 (53.5)	165,563 (54.5)	171,502 (53.9)	174,791 (52.4)	175,891 (50.3)

(table continues next page)

Table A.1 Argentina: Consolidated public sector debt dynamics (in millions of US dollars) *(continued)*

	1997	1998	1999	2000	2001 (projected)	2002 (projected)	2003 (projected)	2004 (projected)	2005 (projected)
Memorandum items (in millions of pesos, unless otherwise indicated):									
Gross Domestic Product	292,825	298,948	283,260	285,045	291,178	303,605	318,202	333,816	350,009
Real GDP growth (in percent)	8.1	3.8	-3.4	-0.5	2.0	3.7	4.3	4.3	4.3
Federal government balance	-4,677	-3,828	-7,156	-6,974	-6,500	-5,000	-3,500	-1,700	0
Provincial governments balance	-1,379	-2,487	-4,632	-3,231	-2,760	-1,898	-1,039	-389	0
Implicit average interest rate (percent)	6.3	7.0	7.8	8.6	9.6	9.5	9.7	9.9	10.0
Interest rate on new federal government debt (percent)[3]	—	—	—	10.9	10.2	10.6	11.4	10.1	9.7

1. Includes one-off gains made in debt management operations.
2. Includes quasi-fiscal surplus not transferred to the treasury, capitalized interest, and valuation adjustments; in 2001, includes also Arg$400 million for payments due to judicial rulings on ANSES (Argentine Social Security Administration) and Arg$800 million for consolidation of INDER's (National Institute for Reinsurance SE) past obligations. In the projection period the quasi-fiscal surplus is projected at Arg$300 million per annum.
3. Assumes a marginal interest rate on market operations of 13 percent in 2001 and declining by 50 basis points every year thereafter.

Note: Figures in parentheses are in percent of GDP.

Sources: IMF Country Report No. 01/90 (June 2001).

critical difference between responsible, professional analysis that honestly attempts to assess central tendencies and reasonable bounds of uncertainty and advocacy analysis that endeavors to support a precooked conclusion favored by a country's authorities and Fund management. In the post-Enron era, when private-sector auditors and analysts are—properly in my view—being held to reasonable standards of professional integrity, the Fund's Executive Board should consider whether it should accept substantially less from Fund staff and management.

Index

interest rates, US
  Argentine rates compared with, 21, 34
  cuts in, 36
  US Treasuries, 1, 33–35, 40, 41, 49
internal debt, Argentine. *See* sovereign debt,
  Argentine; sovereign internal debt,
  Argentine
international capital markets. *See also* private
  capital markets
  IMF future role, 55–59
  IMF lessons, 74–75
international community. *See also specific elements,
  institutions, and members*
  Argentine economic future, 5, 54, 56–57, 60,
    63–65
  Argentine economic history overview, 1–2
  Argentine financial crisis background, 27–36,
    46–49
  Argentine fiscal policy and IMF, 19, 28
  IMF lessons, 67, 73, 76
  ownership of IMF-supported programs, 7
international credit markets. *See* international
  financial markets
international economic system
  IMF future role, 57, 65
  IMF lessons, 5, 67–69
international financial institutions, 56, 58–59. *See
  also specific institutions*
international financial markets. *See also* foreign
  investors
  Argentine economic future, 65
  Argentine economic history overview, 1, 4
  Argentine financial crisis background, 25–33,
    35–44, 49
  Argentine fiscal policy and IMF, 19
  Argentine fiscal policy sustainability issues, 17
  IMF lessons, 68, 75
International Monetary Fund (IMF)
  abolition of as option, 73
  accountability of Fund as issue, 69–70, 81
  area departments and bias, 69–70
  Argentine economic future, 5, 54–65
  Argentine economic history overview, 1–6
  Argentine financial crisis background, 26–51
  Argentine fiscal failures, 17–20, 69, 71
  Argentine fiscal policy sustainability issues, 4,
    12, 69, 74
  Argentine payment schedule, 56, 56*t*
  Argentine sovereign debt dynamics analysis,
    38, 77–81, 79–80*t*
  Articles of Agreement, 24, 39
  bias issues, 69–71, 81
  conditionality (*See* conditionality)
  Country Report 01/90, 38, 77–81
  "exceptional circumstances" terminology, 72
  Executive Board
    accountability of Fund as issue, 70, 81
    IMF key role tensions, 68
    large financial support role, 71, 72
    and "law of the Fund", 38*n*

policies and procedures overview, 42–43
Stand-By Arrangement approval, 4, 36, 38,
  38*n*, 71
"extraordinary financing" by, 57–58
General Agreements to Borrow, 43
IMF-World Bank Annual Meeting, 2, 19, 51–52
independent evaluation office role, 70, 72
International Monetary and Finance Committee
  deliberations, 29, 32–33, 54
key role tensions, 67–69
large financial support role, 3–5, 30–33, 33*n*, 36,
  43–44, 48, 55–59, 65, 68, 71–76
"law of the Fund", 38*n*
lending into arrears by, 57, 58
lessons for, 3–5, 7, 67–76
Letters of Intent to the Fund, 42
managing director role, 42–43
ownership issues, 7
performance of Fund as issue, 48, 69–71
policies and procedures overview, 42–43
program review requirement, 44
rollover of existing support, 58, 65
rollover of repayments, 56, 57
as social worker, 67–69
Supplemental Reserve Facility, 55
three monkeys assessment approach, 44
as tough cop, 67–68
uniformity of treatment principle, 31–32, 56,
  58
international reserves. *See* foreign exchange
  reserves, Argentine

Korea, South. *See* South Korea

labor markets, Argentine
  and Convertibility Plan, 23–24
  inflexibility of, 9
labor unions, Argentine, and Convertibility Plan,
  23
large financial support, IMF role. *See* International
  Monetary Fund
legal issues, Argentine. *See also* Congress,
  Argentine
  bankruptcy law, 53
  collection actions, 29
  disrespect for rule of law, 52, 60
  economic subversion law, 53
  fiscal responsibility law, 77
  funds transfer to provinces, 16
Lenicov, Remes, 54
long-term instruments
  Argentine economic history overview, 1
  Argentine financial crisis background, 26
  IMF lessons, 74
Lopez-Murphy, Ricardo, 36–37

Machinea, Luis, 36
media
  on Argentine crisis, 5
  Argentine government leaks to, 41

privatization, Argentine
of banks, 20–21
success of, 51
privatization receipts, Argentine
fiscal policy and IMF, 15–16, 17
fiscal policy sustainability issues, 14
IMF analysis of sovereign debt dynamics, 79*t*
provincial debt, Argentine
changes in, 80*t*
Duhalde administration policy, 54
economic future and IMF, 60–61
economic history overview, 6
financial crisis background, 31, 37, 49
fiscal policy sustainability issues, 14
provincial governments, transfers to
delays in, 41, 44
legal requirement for, 16
temporary reduction in, 54
public debt, Argentine. *See specific headings beginning with* sovereign debt

real exchange rate, Argentine
changes in, 18, 21, 23*f*, 62, 78
real gross domestic product (GDP), Argentine
changes in, 10–17, 11*f*, 12*t*, 13*f*, 45, 79*t*
projections for, 60
real interest rates, rise in, 45
Real Plan, 25. *See also* Brazilian crisis; exchange rate policy, Brazilian
recessions, Argentine
and Brazilian crisis, 9
economic history overview, 1, 2
financial crisis background, 26, 28, 31, 35–37, 42, 44, 50, 51
fiscal policy sustainability issues, 10, 12, 14, 17, 19
IMF analysis of sovereign debt dynamics, 78
reform efforts. *See* economic policy, Argentine; *specific types of policy*
Report of the International Financial Institutions Advisor Commission, 73–74
reserves, Argentine. *See also* foreign exchange reserves, Argentine
Convertibility Plan requirement, 20
economic future and IMF, 58, 62
revenues, of Argentine government. *See* government revenues, Argentine
Rua, Fernando de la. *See* de la Rua, Fernando
Russia
Argentine fiscal policy and IMF, 20
IMF assistance to, 3, 43, 48
IMF lessons, 75, 76

Saa, Rodriguez, 53
savings, changes in value of, 23
Schröder, Gerhard, 47
servicing of debt. *See* sovereign external debt servicing, Argentine
short-term instruments
Argentine financial crisis background, 25–27
IMF lessons, 74, 75

social consensus. *See* people, Argentine; popular opinion
societal changes, Argentine, 23–24
South Korea, IMF assistance to, 3, 48, 76
sovereign bondholders. *See* bondholders
sovereign bond spreads. *See* interest rate spreads, Argentine bonds
sovereign debt, Argentine. *See also* provincial debt, Argentine
changes in total public debt, 12*t*, 17
and Convertibility Plan reserve requirement, 20
debt-GDP ratio, 10, 12*t*, 14–17, 27, 34–35, 45, 77–78
debt swap, 39–41
financial crisis background, 25–28
IMF analysis of, 38, 77–81, 79–80*t*
IMF payment schedule, 56, 56*t*
IMF Stand-By Arrangement approval, 4, 36, 38, 38*n*, 71
rollover by domestic holders, 27
rollover of existing support, 58
rollover of repayments, 56, 57
sovereign external debt default, Argentine
economic history overview, 2, 4, 6
financial crisis background, 26–39, 43, 46–52
fiscal policy sustainability issues, 10
IMF future role, 55–58, 64–65
IMF lessons, 71, 73–76
ratification of, 53
sovereign external debt rescheduling, Argentine, 49
sovereign external debt restructuring, Argentine
economic history overview, 6
financial crisis background, 29–30, 32–33, 36, 44, 50
fiscal policy sustainability issues, 10, 14–17
IMF lessons, 73
sovereign external debt servicing, Argentine. *See also* interest expenses, Argentine; principal expenses, Argentine
economic history overview, 4, 9
financial crisis background, 27, 29, 40–41, 49
fiscal policy sustainability issues, 16
IMF future role, 57–58, 60, 60*n*, 63, 63*n*
suspension of, 53
sovereign external debt servicing (in general), IMF practices, 59
sovereign internal debt, Argentine. *See also* sovereign debt, Argentine
financial crisis background, 26–27, 30, 40
fiscal policy sustainability issues, 10
IMF future role, 60, 62
Spain
Argentine financial crisis background, 31
privatization of Argentine banks, 20
spending, by Argentine government. *See* government spending, Argentine
stabilization efforts. *See* economic policy, Argentine; *specific types of policy*

Other Publications from the Institute for International Economics

* = out of print

Korea in the World Economy*   Il SaKong
January 1993   ISBN 0-88132-183-4
Pacific Dynamism and the International
Economic System*
C. Fred Bergsten and Marcus Noland, editors
May 1993   ISBN 0-88132-196-6
Economic Consequences of Soviet Disintegration*
John Williamson, editor
May 1993   ISBN 0-88132-190-7
Reconcilable Differences? United States-Japan
Economic Conflict*
C. Fred Bergsten and Marcus Noland
June 1993   ISBN 0-88132-129-X
Does Foreign Exchange Intervention Work?
Kathryn M. Dominguez and Jeffrey A. Frankel
September 1993   ISBN 0-88132-104-4
Sizing Up U.S. Export Disincentives*
J. David Richardson
September 1993   ISBN 0-88132-107-9
NAFTA: An Assessment
Gary Clyde Hufbauer and Jeffrey J. Schott/*rev. ed.*
October 1993   ISBN 0-88132-199-0
Adjusting to Volatile Energy Prices
Philip K. Verleger, Jr.
November 1993   ISBN 0-88132-069-2
The Political Economy of Policy Reform
John Williamson, editor
January 1994   ISBN 0-88132-195-8
Measuring the Costs of Protection
in the United States
Gary Clyde Hufbauer and Kimberly Ann Elliott
January 1994   ISBN 0-88132-108-7
The Dynamics of Korean Economic Development*
Cho Soon
March 1994   ISBN 0-88132-162-1
Reviving the European Union*
C. Randall Henning, Eduard Hochreiter, and Gary
Clyde Hufbauer, editors
April 1994   ISBN 0-88132-208-3
China in the World Economy   Nicholas R. Lardy
April 1994   ISBN 0-88132-200-8
Greening the GATT: Trade, Environment, and the
Future   Daniel C. Esty
July 1994   ISBN 0-88132-205-9
Western Hemisphere Economic Integration*
Gary Clyde Hufbauer and Jeffrey J. Schott
July 1994   ISBN 0-88132-159-1
Currencies and Politics in the United States,
Germany, and Japan
C. Randall Henning
September 1994   ISBN 0-88132-127-3
Estimating Equilibrium Exchange Rates
John Williamson, editor
September 1994   ISBN 0-88132-076-5
Managing the World Economy: Fifty Years After
Bretton Woods   Peter B. Kenen, editor
September 1994   ISBN 0-88132-212-1

Reciprocity and Retaliation in U.S. Trade Policy
Thomas O. Bayard and Kimberly Ann Elliott
September 1994   ISBN 0-88132-084-6
The Uruguay Round: An Assessment*
Jeffrey J. Schott, assisted by Johanna W. Buurman
November 1994   ISBN 0-88132-206-7
Measuring the Costs of Protection in Japan*
Yoko Sazanami, Shujiro Urata, and Hiroki Kawai
January 1995   ISBN 0-88132-211-3
Foreign Direct Investment in the United States,
3rd Ed.   Edward M. Graham and Paul R. Krugman
January 1995   ISBN 0-88132-204-0
The Political Economy of Korea-United States
Cooperation*
C. Fred Bergsten and Il SaKong, editors
February 1995   ISBN 0-88132-213-X
International Debt Reexamined*   William R. Cline
February 1995   ISBN 0-88132-083-8
American Trade Politics, 3rd Ed.   I.M. Destler
April 1995   ISBN 0-88132-215-6
Managing Official Export Credits: The Quest for a
Global Regime*   John E. Ray
July 1995   ISBN 0-88132-207-5
Asia Pacific Fusion: Japan's Role in APEC*
Yoichi Funabashi
October 1995   ISBN 0-88132-224-5
Korea-United States Cooperation in the New
World Order*
C. Fred Bergsten and Il SaKong, editors
February 1996   ISBN 0-88132-226-1
Why Exports Really Matter! * ISBN 0-88132-221-0
Why Exports Matter More!* ISBN 0-88132-229-6
J. David Richardson and Karin Rindal
July 1995; February 1996
Global Corporations and National Governments
Edward M. Graham
May 1996   ISBN 0-88132-111-7
Global Economic Leadership and the Group of
Seven   C. Fred Bergsten and C. Randall Henning
May 1996   ISBN 0-88132-218-0
The Trading System After the Uruguay Round*
John Whalley and Colleen Hamilton
July 1996   ISBN 0-88132-131-1
Private Capital Flows to Emerging Markets After
the Mexican Crisis*   Guillermo A. Calvo,
Morris Goldstein, and Eduard Hochreiter
September 1996   ISBN 0-88132-232-6
The Crawling Band as an Exchange Rate Regime:
Lessons from Chile, Colombia, and Israel
John Williamson
September 1996   ISBN 0-88132-231-8
Flying High: Liberalizing Civil Aviation in the
Asia Pacific*
Gary Clyde Hufbauer and Christopher Findlay
November 1996   ISBN 0-88132-227-X
Measuring the Costs of Visible Protection in
Korea*   Namdoo Kim
November 1996   ISBN 0-88132-236-9

The World Trading System: Challenges Ahead
Jeffrey J. Schott
December 1996   ISBN 0-88132-235-0
Has Globalization Gone Too Far?   Dani Rodrik
March 1997   ISBN cloth 0-88132-243-1
Korea-United States Economic Relationship*
C. Fred Bergsten and Il SaKong, editors
March 1997   ISBN 0-88132-240-7
Summitry in the Americas: A Progress Report
Richard E. Feinberg
April 1997   ISBN 0-88132-242-3
Corruption and the Global Economy
Kimberly Ann Elliott
June 1997   ISBN 0-88132-233-4
Regional Trading Blocs in the World Economic
System   Jeffrey A. Frankel
October 1997   ISBN 0-88132-202-4
Sustaining the Asia Pacific Miracle:
Environmental Protection and Economic
Integration   André Dua and Daniel C. Esty
October 1997   ISBN 0-88132-250-4
Trade and Income Distribution   William R. Cline
November 1997   ISBN 0-88132-216-4
Global Competition Policy
Edward M. Graham and J. David Richardson
December 1997   ISBN 0-88132-166-4
Unfinished Business: Telecommunications after
the Uruguay Round
Gary Clyde Hufbauer and Erika Wada
December 1997   ISBN 0-88132-257-1
Financial Services Liberalization in the WTO
Wendy Dobson and Pierre Jacquet
June 1998   ISBN 0-88132-254-7
Restoring Japan's Economic Growth
Adam S. Posen
September 1998   ISBN 0-88132-262-8
Measuring the Costs of Protection in China
Zhang Shuguang, Zhang Yansheng, and Wan
Zhongxin
November 1998   ISBN 0-88132-247-4
Foreign Direct Investment and Development: The
New Policy Agenda for Developing Countries and
Economies in Transition
Theodore H. Moran
December 1998   ISBN 0-88132-258-X
Behind the Open Door: Foreign Enterprises in the
Chinese Marketplace
Daniel H. Rosen
January 1999   ISBN 0-88132-263-6
Toward A New International Financial
Architecture: A Practical Post-Asia Agenda
Barry Eichengreen
February 1999   ISBN 0-88132-270-9
Is the U.S. Trade Deficit Sustainable?
Catherine L. Mann/ September 1999
ISBN 0-88132-265-2

Safeguarding Prosperity in a Global Financial
System: The Future International Financial
Architecture, Independent Task Force Report
Sponsored by the Council on Foreign Relations
Morris Goldstein, Project Director
October 1999   ISBN 0-88132-287-3
Avoiding the Apocalypse: The Future of the
Two Koreas   Marcus Noland
June 2000   ISBN 0-88132-278-4
Assessing Financial Vulnerability: An Early
Warning System for Emerging Markets
Morris Goldstein, Graciela Kaminsky, and
Carmen Reinhart
June 2000   ISBN 0-88132-237-7
Global Electronic Commerce: A Policy Primer
Catherine L. Mann, Sue E. Eckert, and Sarah
Cleeland Knight
July 2000   ISBN 0-88132-274-1
The WTO after Seattle   Jeffrey J. Schott, editor
July 2000   ISBN 0-88132-290-3
Intellectual Property Rights in the Global
Economy   Keith E. Maskus
August 2000   ISBN 0-88132-282-2
The Political Economy of the Asian Financial
Crisis   Stephan Haggard
August 2000   ISBN 0-88132-283-0
Transforming Foreign Aid: United States
Assistance in the 21st Century   Carol Lancaster
August 2000   ISBN 0-88132-291-1
Fighting the Wrong Enemy: Antiglobal Activists
and Multinational Enterprises   Edward M.Graham
September 2000   ISBN 0-88132-272-5
Globalization and the Perceptions of American
Workers
Kenneth F. Scheve and Matthew J. Slaughter
March 2001   ISBN 0-88132-295-4
World Capital Markets: Challenge to the G-10
Wendy Dobson and Gary C. Hufbauer,
assisted by Hyun Koo Cho
May 2001   ISBN 0-88132-301-2
Prospects for Free Trade in the Americas
Jeffrey J. Schott
August 2001   ISBN 0-88132-275-X
Lessons from the Old World for the New:
Constructing a North American Community
Robert A. Pastor
August 2001   ISBN 0-88132-328-4
Measuring the Costs of Protection in Europe:
European Commercial Policy in the 2000s
Patrick A. Messerlin
September 2001   ISBN 0-88132-273-3
Job Loss from Imports: Measuring the Costs
Lori G. Kletzer
September 2001   ISBN 0-88132-296-2
No More Bashing: Building a New Japan-United
States Economic Relationship
C. Fred Bergsten, Takatoshi Ito, and Marc Noland
October 2001   ISBN 0-88132-286-5

Why Global Commitment Really Matters!
Howard Lewis III and J. David Richardson
October 2001 ISBN 0-88132-298-9
Leadership Selection in the Major Multilaterals
Miles Kahler
November 2001 ISBN 0-88132-335-7
**The International Financial Architecture:
What's New? What's Missing?** Peter Kenen
November 2001 ISBN 0-88132-297-0
**Delivering on Debt Relief: From IMF Gold to
a New Aid Architecture**
John Williamson and Nancy Birdsall,
with Brian Deese
April 2002 ISBN 0-88132-331-4

10 **Economic Integration of the Korean Peninsula**
Marcus Noland, editor
January 1998 ISBN 0-88132-255-5
11 **Restarting Fast Track*** Jeffrey J. Schott, editor
April 1998 ISBN 0-88132-259-8
12 **Launching New Global Trade Talks:
An Action Agenda** Jeffrey J. Schott, editor
September 1998 ISBN 0-88132-266-0
13 **Japan's Financial Crisis and Its Parallels to
US Experience**
Ryoichi Mikitani and Adam S. Posen, eds.
September 2000 ISBN 0-88132-289-X
14 **The Ex-Im Bank in the 21st Century: A New
Approach?** Gary Clyde Hufbauer and
Rita M. Rodriguez, eds.
January 2001 ISBN 0-88132-300-4

SPECIAL REPORTS

1 **Promoting World Recovery: A Statement on
Global Economic Strategy***
by Twenty-six Economists from Fourteen
Countries
December 1982 ISBN 0-88132-013-7
2 **Prospects for Adjustment in Argentina,
Brazil, and Mexico: Responding to the Debt
Crisis*** John Williamson, editor
June 1983 ISBN 0-88132-016-1
3 **Inflation and Indexation: Argentina, Brazil,
and Israel*** John Williamson, editor
March 1985 ISBN 0-88132-037-4
4 **Global Economic Imbalances***
C. Fred Bergsten, editor
March 1986 ISBN 0-88132-042-0
5 **African Debt and Financing***
Carol Lancaster and John Williamson, editors
May 1986 ISBN 0-88132-044-7
6 **Resolving the Global Economic Crisis: After
Wall Street***
by Thirty-three Economists from Thirteen
Countries
December 1987 ISBN 0-88132-070-6
7 **World Economic Problems***
Kimberly Ann Elliott and John Williamson,
editors
April 1988 ISBN 0-88132-055-2
Reforming World Agricultural Trade*
by Twenty-nine Professionals from Seventeen
Countries
1988 ISBN 0-88132-088-9
8 **Economic Relations Between the United
States and Korea: Conflict or Cooperation?***
Thomas O. Bayard and Soo-Gil Young, editors
January 1989 ISBN 0-88132-068-4
9 **Whither APEC? The Progress to Date and
Agenda for the Future***
C. Fred Bergsten, editor
October 1997 ISBN 0-88132-248-2

WORKS IN PROGRESS

**Deunionization in the United States:
The Role of International Trade**
Robert E. Baldwin
**Changing Direction: The New Economy
in the United States, Europe, and Japan**
Martin Baily
**New Regional Arrangements and the World
Economy**
C. Fred Bergsten
**The Globalization Backlash in Europe and the
United States**
C. Fred Bergsten, Pierre Jacquet, and Karl Kaiser
**Globalization and Its Consequences for Poverty,
Inequality, and Growth**
Surjit Bhalla
Korea Diaspora in the World Economy
Inbom Choi, editor
China's Entry to the World Economy
Richard N. Cooper
The ILO in the World Economy
Kimberly Ann Elliott
**Can Labor Standards Improve Under
Globalization?**
Kimberly Ann Elliott and Richard B. Freeman
Reforming Economic Sanctions
Kimberly Ann Elliott, Gary C. Hufbauer, and
Jeffrey J. Schott
Free Trade in Labor Agency Services
Kimberly Ann Elliott and J. David Richardson
IMF and the World Bank
Michael Fabricius
The Chaebol and Structural Problems in Korea
Edward M. Graham
East Asian Financial Cooperation
E. Randall Henning
Managing Trade Conflicts in Food Safety
Timothy Josling, David Orden, and Donna Roberts

DISTRIBUTORS OUTSIDE THE UNITED STATES

Australia, New Zealand, and Papua New Guinea
D.A. Information Services
648 Whitehorse Road
Mitcham, Victoria 3132, Australia
tel: 61-3-9210-7777
fax: 61-3-9210-7788
e-mail: service@dadirect.com.au
http://www.dadirect.com.au

Canada
Renouf Bookstore
5369 Canotek Road, Unit 1
Ottawa, Ontario K1J 9J3, Canada
tel: 613-745-2665
fax: 613-745-7660
http://www.renoufbooks.com

United Kingdom and Europe
(including Russia and Turkey)
The Eurospan Group
3 Henrietta Street, Covent Garden
London WC2E 8LU England
tel: 44-20-7240-0856
fax: 44-20-7379-0609
http://www.eurospan.co.uk

India, Bangladesh, Nepal, and Sri Lanka
Viva Books Pvt.
Mr. Vinod Vasishtha
4325/3, Ansari Rd.
Daryaganj, New Delhi-110002
India
tel: 91-11-327-9280
fax: 91-11-326-7224
e-mail: vinod.viva@gndel.globalnet.
ems.vsnl.net.in

Japan and the Republic of Korea
United Publishers Services, Ltd.
Kenkyu-Sha Bldg.
9, Kanda Surugadai 2-Chome
Chiyoda-Ku, Tokyo 101
Japan
tel: 81-3-3291-4541
fax: 81-3-3292-8610
e-mail: saito@ups.co.jp
For trade accounts only.
Individuals will find IIE books in leading Tokyo bookstores.

Southeast Asia (Brunei, Cambodia, China, Malaysia, Hong Kong, Indonesia, Laos, Myanmar, the Philippines, Singapore, Taiwan, and Vietnam)
Hemisphere Publication Services
1 Kallang Pudding Rd. #04-03
Golden Wheel Building
Singapore 349316
tel: 65-741-5166
fax: 65-742-9356

Thailand
Asia Books
5 Sukhumvit Rd. Soi 61
Bangkok 10110 Thailand
tel: 662-714-0740-2 Ext: 221, 222, 223
fax: 662-391-2277
e-mail: purchase@asiabooks.co.th
http://www/asiabooksonline.com

Visit our Web site at:
http://www.iie.com
E-mail orders to:
orders@iie.com